MUSBURY AND ALDEN

Seven hundred years of life and landscape

MUSBURY AND ALDEN

Seven hundred years of life and landscape

JOHN SIMPSON

HELMSHORE LOCAL HISTORY SOCIETY

2008

First published 2008
Helmshore Local History Society

ISBN 978-0-906881-19-4

Designed and typeset by :
Croft Publications, 8 St James Meadow,
Boroughbridge, YO51 9NW

Printed and bound by :
Smith Settle
Gateway Drive, Yeadon,
West Yorkshire LS19 7XY

CONTENTS

For Jane

PREFACE

Visitors to Helmshore may sometimes have wondered why one small area of the village boasts a Park Street, Park Road, Park House and Park Mill, and why the church is known as Musbury Parish Church and not Helmshore Parish Church. The answer lies in events that began some seven hundred years ago and more when Henry de Lacy, Earl of Lincoln, set aside a remote corner of his Lancashire estates as a deer park. Remarkably, the memory of this enterprise survives not just in place names, but also in physical remains, which we can still see on the ground today.

The following pages trace the history of the deer park and the changes it underwent following its demise. In the 16th century, it became the home of farmers and textile workers who carved it up into the farms and fields we see today. Their place was taken by 18th and 19th century industrialists who left their own mark on landscape's page.

I am very grateful to the staffs of all the record offices and libraries I have visited in the course of research for the book. I would also like to thank Chris Aspin, Carol and Fred Barlow, Mike Clarke, Eddie Roberts, Diana Winterbotham and Lawrence Witham for their help.

John Simpson,
Helmshore

WITHIN THE PALE

A GREAT UNDERTAKING

THE YEAR is 1305 and in the wooded valleys of Musbury and Alden, there is great activity. Labourers are busy digging out a huge ditch and throwing up the earth to raise a bank above it. When complete, it will encircle most of the two valleys. Elsewhere, carpenters cut and shape lengths of oak timber, which they drive into the ground and fasten together with rails to form a long fence around the outside of the ditch. Meanwhile, teams of oxen slowly drag more timber from nearby woods as raw material for the new fence.[1]

All of this work was taking place on the order of Henry de Lacy, Earl of Lincoln, who owned the manors of Accrington and Tottington, as well as huge tracts of land elsewhere in the north of England. He had decided to set aside one corner of his vast estate as an enclosure in which to keep deer. This would allow him and his followers to hunt the animals whenever they happened to be in the area, while at other times the deer park would operate almost as a 'deer farm', supplying venison for the Earl's table.

De Lacy was one of the most powerful men in England in 1305. He was born in 1249 and had succeeded his father when aged just eight-and-a-half. He became a close and trusted friend and servant of Edward I and campaigned with him against the Welsh and Scots. Following Edward's death, de Lacy continued in his role as elder statesman and advisor to the new king Edward II, until his own death in 1311.[2]

The years on either side of 1300 were the heyday of the medieval deer park. In total, there were some 3,200 of them, covering something like two per cent of the English countryside. They were status symbols, which only the well-to-do could afford. Their size varied enormously, the smallest covering only a few acres, while the largest enclosed over 1,000 acres. As befitted a park belonging to one of the most powerful and richest men in the land, Musbury park extended to about 1,713 acres.[3]

We know something of the park's construction because of the chance survival of a set of the Earl's accounts or *compoti* covering the period from the end of September 1304 to the end of September in the following year. These accounts were drawn up by two men who acted as receivers for the Earl. Simon Noel's period in office ran from 30th September 1304 to 30th March 1305 and his successor, Robert, son of Adam, held the post from the beginning of April to the end of September 1305.

The land that formed the deer park was originally part of the manor of Tottington and the first indication of the park's construction comes in the

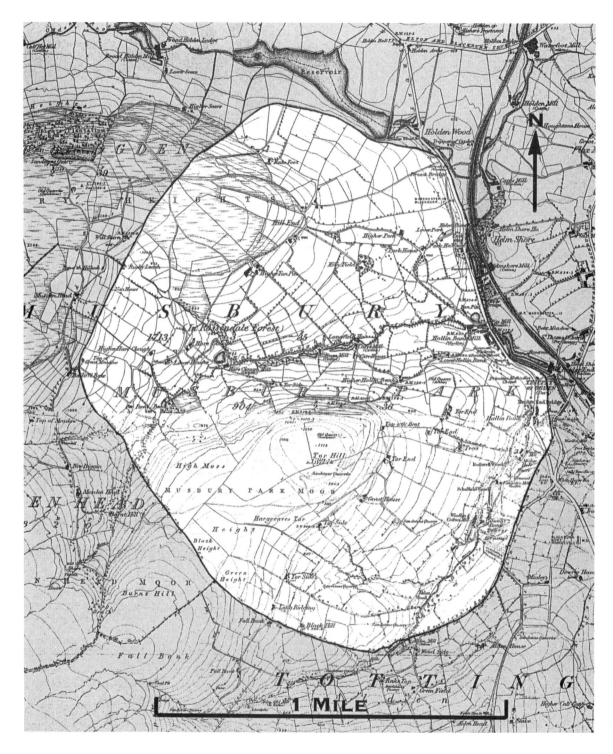

The area enclosed within the deer park superimposed on the first edition six-inch Ordnance Survey map from the 1840s. As well as Musbury Tor and the Musbury valley, the park included a small part of Grane and the north side of Alden.

expenses in Simon's accounts. He recorded the payment of £22 10s *'to carpenters as part of their wages for felling timber and making a paling in part for the park of Alvedene and Musdene.'* Robert's accounts contain more details, beginning with a receipt of £3 6s 10d for the herbage of *'Aldene, Musdene and Ugdene'*. (This was money paid by local people in return for grazing their animals). He noted that the sum was *'not more on account of the park there newly made.'* In other words, land that had previously provided grazing for cattle had been taken for the deer park so no money could be collected for it. The expenses in the accounts included:

> Making and planting nine hundred, five score and six perches of paling round Musbirry park, with the carriage of the said paling in part from Tottington wood. The rest was done by Simon Noel, as appears in his compotus £60 10s 5¼d
>
> 18 oxen bought for the carriage of the paling £8 17s 9d

The accounts end with a note of a reward given to two hard working carpenters:

> Given by the Earl to William le Wainwright and Richard de Helay makers of the paling of Musbirry park, and specially to them, because they worked better and more than the others £1 0s 0d [4]

We can still trace much of the boundary of Musbury park on the ground today, seven hundred years after its construction. If we begin at the White Horse and walk along Alden Road, once we have passed the junction with Stake Lane, we are following the line of the park ditch. Then from Alden reservoir, the boundary climbs the hillside to Fall Bank where the line of the ditch becomes a deep gully. It crosses Green Height into Musbury near Burnt Hill and then runs down to Musbury Brook, arcs across the opposite hillside to Bailiff's Rake where it turns north-east to Rushy Leach. It is here that the ditch and bank are in their best state of preservation and they can be easily explored since a public footpath follows their line. Musbury Heights quarry destroyed much of the next section of the boundary, but the ditch appears again above Tenements farm in Grane and just south of the Holden Vale Hotel, near Holcombe Road.

The later development of Helmshore obliterated all evidence of the rest of the boundary back to our starting point. However, a strange anomaly in the tenurial history of a row of cottages places precisely one short length of it at Bridge End. Before the abolition of copyhold tenure in 1925, part of the row of houses numbered 25 – 33, Station Road was copyhold and part freehold. The houses had, in fact, been built across the line of the park fence. That part of their site which lay within the old deer park boundary was copyhold, while the rest had been part of land between the fence and the River Ogden granted to the Holdens of Holden Hall and was therefore freehold.[5]

Once complete, Musbury park would have been stocked with fallow deer, which the Normans had introduced into Britain and which were easier to keep in a confined area than native red or roe deer. Inside the park fence there was a mixture

Two views of the park ditch. *(Left)* The line of the ditch at Fall Bank in 1983 and the ruins of Rushy Leach in 1957 with the ditch running up the hillside beyond the house.

of woodland and pasture. Some parks were 'uncompartmented' and deer were allowed to roam freely, but trees were pollarded to allow the timber to grow above the level at which deer could browse. 'Compartmented' parks had clear divisions between areas of woodland (coppices) and areas of grassland with pollarded trees (launds). Musbury was probably a compartmented park, and some of the earthen banks that we can still see on the slopes of the valley may mark these ancient divisions within the park. [6]

While the bank and strong fence around the park's perimeter stopped the deer from escaping, part of the boundary was adapted to allow wild deer to enter the park to keep up stock levels. In October 1323, when Edward II was staying at the manor house at Ightenhill (near Burnley), he ordered that a deer leap or 'saltatory' should be constructed at Musbury at a cost of 18s. This consisted of a section of fence that was lower than the rest and over which deer outside the park could leap. The steep slope inside made it impossible for them to jump back out again. Elsewhere, there was at least one gate in the park pale. We know that there was one in the Alden side of the fence because later one of the fields belonging to Clough farm was called Park Gate Field.[7]

The park also contained a lodge where the parker or park-keeper lived to oversee its day-to-day running. In the early 20th century, Thomas Hayhurst, a Radcliffe historian, suggested to members of the Lancashire and Cheshire Antiquarian Society that Great House in Alden stood on the site of the Musbury park lodge.[8] He made much of the name, saying that it indicated that a building of some significance must have stood there, but in fact it was not the only farm that later stood within the boundaries of the park to which the name was applied. The farm we now know as Higher Tan Pits was also referred to as the 'Great House' in 16th and 17th century manorial records. A lodge on the site of the present Great House farm would have had fine views of the park in Alden , but Tor would have hidden most of the remainder from view. Perhaps a better candidate for the site of the lodge is Park House (either Middle or Higher Park House). The name suggests a long association with the park and we know that it was among the eight farms created when the park was divided up in the early 16th century. Any building at the Park House site would have commanded views of most of Musbury, Tor and its lower slopes, Musbury Heights and the lower boundary of the park near the Ogden. Without a detailed archaeological survey, however, we cannot be sure whether the lodge stood at Park House, Great House or somewhere completely different in the park.

The parker's duties included keeping the fence in repair, protecting the deer from wild animals or poachers, and providing the herd with winter fodder of hay and branches cut from trees in the park. In 1323, his remuneration for these tasks was 1½d per day or 45s 6d a year, but by the late 1400s this had been reduced to 1d a day.[9]

Although the primary purpose of the park was to provide a safe enclosure for the deer, it also had other uses. Some of the underwood could have gone for sale to provide fuel or to make fence posts and implements. Allowing neighbouring farmers to graze their livestock within the park was another source of revenue. For example, in 1323-4, the 'herbage' of Musbury park was sold for 20s, although in the following year the amount was said to be less because a murrain had reduced the number of cattle needing grazing. By 1341–2, when Queen Isabella had taken owner-ship of the park, the grazing of animals within its boundaries raised £6 13s 4d.[10]

COMMON EVILDOERS

The concentration of a herd of deer within a relatively small space proved a great attraction to poachers. This was particularly the case in the turbulent years of the early 1320s. The northern counties had suffered considerably from famine in 1314 – 17 and had been attacked repeatedly by the Scots plundering across the border. The Earl of Lancaster's rebellion against his cousin, Edward II, made matters worse. In the words of G. H. Tupling:

> Armed bands infested the countryside, robbing and ill-treating traders, plundering and burning property. A general spirit of lawlessness prevailed from which no man's person or goods were safe.[11]

The king had to take firm measures to restore law and order. He sent com-missioners into Lancashire to hear complaints, and to indict and try those who had been guilty of various crimes, including hunting and cutting down trees in the king's forests and parks.

In October 1323, two commissioners, Henry le Scrope and Robert de Ayleston, were at Ightenhill hearing evidence. It was recorded that:

> Ithel de Hyndeley, Adam Bletherose, Roger lord of Lytelboulton, Adam Clere of Bury, Gilbert servant of the same Adam, Geoffrey de Klog, Robert le Lytster of Rachedale and Adam Kuck hunted in the park of Musbyry and are common evildoers.

Two other justices, William de Herle and Geoffrey le Scrope, heard that:

> Adam de Radeclyf, John his brother, and Roger brother of Richard the parson of the church of Byry often entered the king's park of Mossebyry and other free chases of the lord king in Blakebourneshire and took and carried away venison ... Robert de Heton, David his brother and Roger de Haywod entered Mossebyry park and the king's other chases of Blakebourneshire and seized and carried off venison.

Adam de Radcliffe pleaded not guilty, but was fined, while Richard de Radcliffe, the parson of Bury was acquitted. Several other men were charged with breaking into the park and catching and destroying all the deer there, but the sheriff could not track them down to bring them to justice.[12]

After the death of Edward II, Musbury park passed to his widow Isabella, but problems with poachers continued. On 1st June, 1337, for example, a commission of oyer and terminer ('to hear and determine') was issued to deal with the cases of more than seventy men who had entered the Queen's free chases *'at Penhill,*

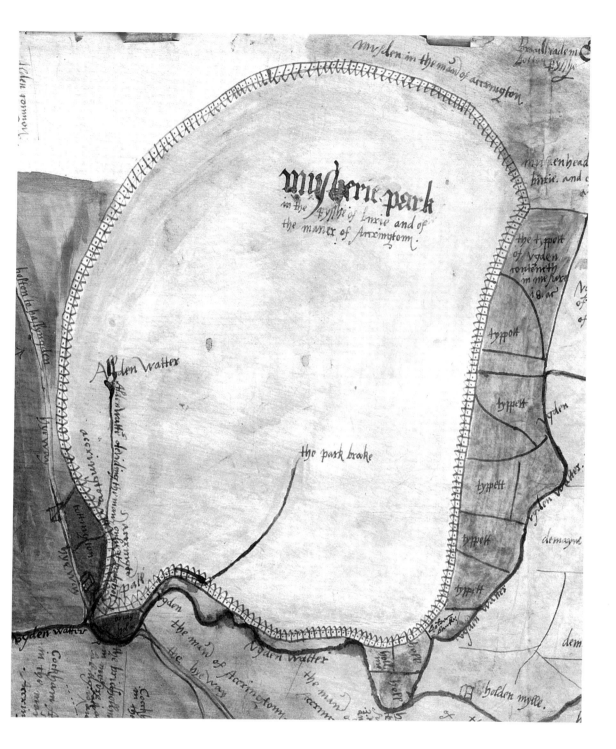

This plan was produced in 1580 following a dispute about the ownership of several pieces of land between the old park boundary and the River Ogden. It shows the fence around the park, although how much of it actually survived at this date is impossible to say.
[*Source: The National Archives MPC1/245*]

Rosceendale and Trouden, and broke her park at Musbury … hunted in these, felled her trees, carried away trees and deer and assaulted her men and servants.'[13]

THE LONG DECLINE

In 1348, Queen Isabella granted Musbury park to Henry, Earl of Lancaster, and thereafter it was once more counted among the possessions of the Duchy. The year was to have a deep significance for the country as a whole since it marked the first visitation of the Black Death. Thousands of people died from the plague in that year and in later epidemics. The resulting labour shortage led to a move away from so-called 'demesne' farming and instead landowners began to rent out their property. Musbury park was no exception. At some date between 1355 and 1361, for instance, Thomas Brownlow, the park-keeper, received a grant of the herbage of the park for eight years.[14] Another lease – this time for ten years – was made to James Radcliffe in 1385. This was the first of a series of leases to the Radcliffes, which saw them holding Musbury park for more than 100 years. They usually paid just over £8 a year in rent. A break in their tenure came in 1467 when Geoffrey Warton took the park for twenty years. His lease stated that he was to repair and maintain the pale, hedges and ditch of the park for all its circuit.[15]

The Duchy of Lancaster continued to appoint park-keepers during this period, but in 1480 a decree ordered that *'no fees nor wages are to be paid to any officer of Musbury Parke, as by Act of Parliament no fees nor wages shall be paid for any office as nedeth nat dayly exercise, and that also in our said parke there is no game to kepe.'*[16] A few years earlier, a description of the park said it was *'a fayre and large grownde febly closed with hegges and noo dere in it.'*[17] The end of the park except in name only was not far off. At the beginning of the 16th century, Henry VII decided to increase the revenue he derived from his forests in the north by abolishing Forest Law and granting land for settlement. In 1507, he ordered that a thorough survey should be made of his lands, including the Forest of Rossendale. The survey reported that:

> There is a Wast ground there callid Musbury park which was sometyme a park in dede and now the closure is downe and is laid to pasture savyng the dere of the foreste of Rossindale hath recorse therin … Whych ground is now by us devided into divers parcell and 8 personnes every man 60 acres wheroff 20 the best, 20 myddyl and 20 of the worst every man to pay for every suche 60 acres 33s 4d. The hole somm emonges theym wyl atteyne to £13 6s 8d wherof let be abatyd … 6s 8d in so moche as there is a lakk emonges them al 10 acres. [18]

A new chapter in Musbury's history had opened.

NOTES

[1] P.A. Lyons (ed), *Two "Compoti" of the Lancashire and Cheshire Manors of Henry de Lacy, Earl of Lincoln, XXIV and XXXIII Edward I*, Chetham Society, Old Series (1884)

[2] *ibid*, pp. v - xvii; J. S. Hamilton, 'Henry de Lacy, Fifth Earl of Lincoln', *Oxford Dictionary of National Biography* [Online edition]

3   Oliver Rackham, *The Illustrated History of the Countryside,* 1994, p.59; L. M. Cantor and J. Hatherly, 'The Medieval Parks of England', *Geography,* 64 (1979) 71 - 85

4   P.A. Lyons, *op.cit.,* pp.175, 177, 185

5   Thomas Woodcock, *Haslingden. A topographical history,* Chetham Society, Third Series (1952), p.44

6   Rackham, *op. cit.,* pp. 59 - 60

7   William Farrer (ed), *Lancashire Inquests, Extents, and Feudal Aids, Part II 1310 - 1333,* Record Society of Lancashire and Cheshire, 54 (1907), p. 201; A survey of lands and premises in the hamlet or township of Musberry, 1793 (LRO: DDX/118/166/1)

8   Patrick Stephens and Richard Hawkin, *Historical Notices of Helmshore and Musbury,* Part II (1929), pp. 33 - 34

9   G. H. Tupling, *The Economic History of Rossendale,* 1927, p. 16

10 William Farrer (ed), *Lancashire Inquests, Extents and Feudal Aids, Part II 1310-1333,* Record Society of Lancashire and Cheshire, 54 (1907), p. 201; R. Cunliffe-Shaw, *The Royal Forest of Lancaster,* 1956, p. 435

11 G. H. Tupling (ed), *South Lancashire in the Reign of Edward II,* Chetham Society, Third Series (1949), p. xxxix

12 G. H. Tupling (ed), *South Lancashire in the Reign of Edward II,* pp. 100 - 110

13 *Calendar of the Patent Rolls preserved in the Public Record Office 1334-1338,* (1895) p. 452

14 *The Thirty Second Annual Report of the Deputy Keeper of the Public Records,* Appendix I, (1871), p. 335

15 Thomas D. Whitaker, *An history of the original parish of Whalley,* 4th edition, volume I, (1872), p. 316

16 Thomas D. Whitaker, *op. cit.,* p. 316 The decree must have been ignored for on 1st October 1485, the office of keeper of the park of Musbury was granted to Laurence Maderer for life with the accustomed fees, wages, etc. (Whitaker, *op. cit.,* p. 316, n. 4)

17 A. R. Myers, 'An official progress through Lancashire and Cheshire in 1476', *Transactions of the Historic Society of Lancashire and Cheshire,* 115 (1963), 26

18 William Farrer (trans), *The court rolls of the Honor of Clitheroe,* Volume II, (1912), p. 373

A NEW BEGINNING

N O LIST survives of the eight people who received a share of Musbury park in 1507, but a rental dating from 1527 must include many of them:

	Copyhold rent		
Adam Halworth [Haworth]	£3	5s	
Richard Dukworth [Duckworth]		46s	8d
The wife of Peter Halworth		32s	6d
Geoffrey Tailior [Taylor]		32s	6d
Laurence Tailior		32s	6d
Otuel Bridge		32s	6d
William Crokeshagh [Cronkshaw]		20s[1]	

Here are the names of the families who were to be associated with Musbury and Alden for several hundred years. Those individuals who were paying a rent of 32s 6d to the Lord of the Manor held one complete eighth share of the old park, while Adam Haworth must have acquired an additional share. Richard Duckworth too had been able to add to his original eighth share, but William Cronkshaw had only a part share of one of the eight parcels. By tracing the changes of ownership of all this land through the manorial court rolls, we can say roughly where the original eight parcels of the park were.

Adam Haworth's two shares centred on Great House and later included not only Great House itself, but also Halliwells, Clough, Black Hill, Trickling Water and Charity. Richard Duckworth's estate comprised the Park House, Kiln Field, Hill End and Rake Foot areas. By 1538 it had been divided up, with the larger share (the Park House lands) going to Richard's son and heir, John, and the Kiln Field part going to his younger son, also called Richard. The second family of Haworths (represented by the wife of Peter Haworth in the 1527 rental) lived at Hollin Bank, while Geoffrey and Lawrence Taylor owned most of the upper end of the Musbury valley, including the land that later formed Higher Tan Pits, Hare Clough, Rushy Leach, Lower Houses and Ferny Bank farms. Ottiwell Bridge's share covered the front flank of Tor at Tor End and William Cronkshaw received land at Hill End (next to Higher Tan Pits).

Several of these properties remained unchanged and in the hands of the same family for generations. Great House, for example, belonged to the Haworths until the 1660s, while the Taylors held on to Higher Tan Pits until 1707. The most extraordinarily long association between one family and one property was that between the Duckworths and Kiln Field. We have seen that Richard Duckworth, junior, received the farm from his father in 1538. Its remaining history is told by a collection of documents that came to light quite by chance.

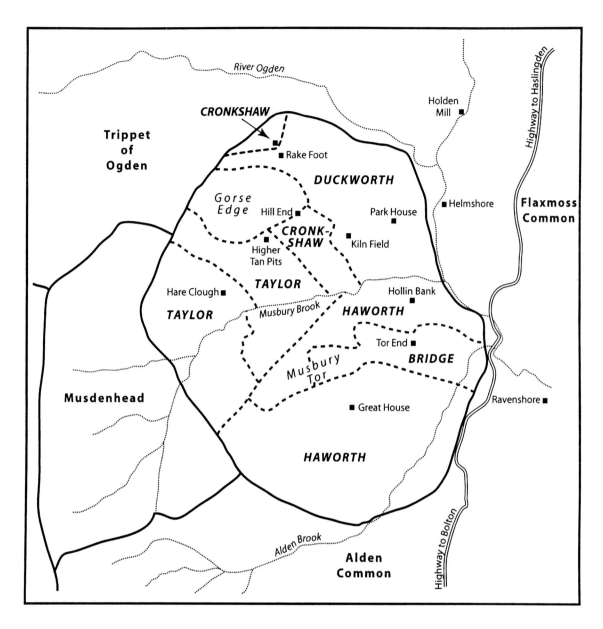

The park in the mid-16th century, showing its division into separate areas belonging to the families named.

One morning in early March 1983, Chris Aspin opened a copy of *The Times* and came across an obituary of Captain Ralph Campbell Musbury Duckworth. Chris knew that Duckworths had been landowners in Musbury for a long time and wondered if Captain Duckworth's family had connections with the valley. He contacted the Captain's brother Arthur who was living at Frome in Somerset and who confirmed that indeed the family had originated from Musbury and that Ralph had been given Musbury as a name to commemorate the link. The family had continued to own farms in Musbury until well into the 20th century and had kept in their family muniments a collection of deeds which give a complete history of Kiln Field and Rake Foot (in the Grane side of the old Musbury township).

The earliest deed among these documents (which are now in the Somerset Record Office) dates from 1538 and records Richard Duckworth's acquisition of Kiln Field, then a farm of some twenty-four customary acres (about fifty statute acres). It passed from father to son through the 16th, 17th and 18th centuries and remained the family home until the 1770s. When George Duckworth, the great-great-great-great-grandson of the original owner, died in about 1779, the farm went to his son, another George, who had taken up law. He was living in The Strand at the time of his father's death, but by the 1790s was practising in Manchester. His business flourished, allowing him to buy property in Chorlton Row (Manchester) and Darwen to add to the Musbury estate. He died in 1815 following a fall from his horse and his will gives us some idea of just how wealthy he had become for it includes bequests of £16,000 each to his daughters Eliza and Anna. The Musbury property went to his son Samuel who in turn bequeathed it to William, his brother, who was the great-grandfather of Ralph Campbell Musbury Duckworth. William's daughter married Sir Henry Newbolt who portrayed him in the novel *The Old Country* as Joe Earnshaw '*a north country lawyer's son, rock-jawed and iron-handed.*'[2]

The Somerset deeds also recount the history of Rake Foot farm. One document dating from 1589 refers to an area of Musbury called Gorse Edge. This seems to have been the flank of Musbury Heights from Hare Clough to Hill End and into Grane above Rake Foot. Patches of gorse still grow on this hillside. The 1589 document is an agreement about access through Gorse Edge to get at peat on the moor. The three signatories to the deed decided that they could all use a way that was to begin '*att a stone pitt on the top of the said Gorse Edge*' and then follow a stone wall, which divided the lands of William Entwistle (part of Park House) and Thomas Duckworth (Kiln Field). Thomas Duckworth was to have the right to use the way not only to fetch peat for his house, but also to get to '*that new howse lately builded by the said Thomas Duckeworth in the said Gorse edge.*' This was Rake Foot farm, which stands overlooking Holden Wood Reservoir. It was rebuilt in 1718 by George Duckworth who set his initials on a datestone there.[3]

All of the Musbury farms would have had a set of records like those for Kiln Field and Rake Foot. Each deed was a copy of an entry from the records of the manor of Accrington and it is through these vellum rolls that we are able to trace the history of the other farms. Some of the 1507 parcels were split up, pieces were sold off or the land divided between different family members. William Cronkshaw was able to increase the amount of land he owned in this way in 1554 when he bought from Richard Duckworth, junior, a house with 20 '*le roode falles*' near it and four acres on Gorse Edge.[4] This farm stood at Rake Foot.

Ottiwell Bridge's share of the old park went through a long process of subdivision. In 1530, it consisted of the original sixty customary acres of land with

This earth bank and ditch mark the boundary between two of the parcels into which the park was divided in 1507. To the left was land belonging to the Cronkshaws at Hill End, while the Taylors at Higher Tan Pits owned the land to the right. In the distance are Carr Lane and Higher Hollin Bank.

John Holden's 'New House' at Tor End, which he built in 1731.
The photograph dates from about 1905.

one farmhouse, probably on the site of the present-day Tor End farm. Christopher and Francis, Ottiwell's sons, each received one half of the property and by 1577, one of them had built a new farmhouse on his land. This may have been the predecessor of the farm known as the Castle or Mansion at Tor End. By 1607, a third farm (now called Trees) shared part of the land. There were no further additions until the early 18th century, when the owner of Trees farm, Edmund Duckworth, built a cottage at Top o' th' Bent, just beneath Tor. At about the same time, John Holden, the owner of the original Tor End farm, divided up his land and built a new farmhouse putting a datestone on it in 1731. This meant that the land, which in 1530 had supported one farmstead, now had five houses on it.[5]

MUSDENHEAD

Outside the park boundary, but closely associated with the park by its very proximity was the former pasture of Musden and Ugden. For much of the 15th century it had been in the hands of the heirs of one Thomas Holden who paid a rent of 15s for it.[6] By 1527 it was shared by Ellis Rothwell and Christopher Hargreaves, but in 1560, it was in the sole ownership of George Nevell from Nottinghamshire. When he sold it in 1566 to Sir William Davenport of Bramhall, there was just one house there. Shortly after 1579, Sir William Davenport's son (also called William) who had inherited the Musdenhead property began to lease small pieces of land there to various tenants. The copyhold rent payable to the Lord of the Manor for these landholdings was just 4d each, which shows they all contained only about one customary acre of land. On the death of the second William Davenport in 1588 the property reverted to his son, another William, and the records of the transfer show that most of the pieces of land leased out between 1579 and 1588 now had a house and outbuildings standing on them.[7]

Some of these farms and cottages must have been short-lived, but others were the origin of the farmsteads whose ruins still stand in Musdenhead. In 1607, for instance, William Davenport sold one of his farms to Lawrence Taylor and the entry in the court rolls recording the sale shows that the farm had several fields with distinctive names, including limestone hey and grandham hey. These names remained in use for several hundred years and were marked on a sale plan in 1884 which shows that the farm was in fact Bailiff's Rake.[8] Similarly, at Easter 1627 when Roger Taylor rented one of the Musdenhead farms, its land included '*a parcel of rough land called le brunt hill adjoining to le mosse land of Alden, Edgworth and Broadhead lying in Musdenhead.*' The remains of this farm – Burnt Hill – still form a substantial ruin at the very head of the valley.[9]

The ruins of Burnt Hill at Musdenhead in the 1950s. The name refers to the process of clearing the moorland by setting fire to its rough vegetation.

The enclosure of most of Alden took place much later than Musbury park. Nearly all of the valley south of the brook and also the Fall Bank area was outside the park boundary and in the Middle Ages was used as grazing for the cattle of people living nearby. By the 16th century, it had been set aside as common land for the use of people in the manor of Tottington (whose northern boundary reached what is now the Bridge End area of Helmshore). The manorial court rolls contain several instances of breaches of the regulations governing the use of this common. In 1526, for instance, Edward Worsseley was fined 4d *'for chasing his neighbours' sheep out of Alden common pasture'*, while in 1567, William Tailior of Musbury was fined for *'unlawfully harrying'* the cattle of the Queen's tenants in Alden and for keeping his hedges open. Robert Gryme and Robert Yait were fined 4d apiece in 1540 for cutting and felling an oak tree growing on the common.[10]

Alden remained in common use until the early 17th century when it was divided up between the main manorial tenants as part of the settlement of the so-called 'Copyhold Dispute.' James I had needed to raise money and had called into question the validity of the way in which people in his manors in East Lancashire held their property. They had to pay to have rights to their land firmly established, but in return, they could enclose large areas of common. All of the main landholders in the manor of Tottington received a share of Alden common, those with the largest property getting the largest allotment in Alden. The common was divided into four large areas called lowmost dole, middle dole, uppermost dole and Foebank dole and land was apportioned out from each dole. Since most of the allotments were too small to be of much use or were too far away from most of the farms in the manor, there quickly grew up a market in the shares of land.[11]

By buying up small shares next to each other in one of the four doles, speculators found that they eventually had enough land to make it worth their while enclosing it and starting a new farm. This is how Cronkshaw Fold began life. The process of its creation started in 1625 when Gilbert Holden sold his share in the lowmost dole to Christopher Cronkshaw of Musbury. A few years later, Cronkshaw bought another piece of lowmost dole from Henry Cowpe of Alderbottom. The two shares together gave him sufficient land to start a farm and he built a house on it in 1631, setting his initials on a datestone. He acquired a third piece of lowmost dole from Richard Holden of Ravenshore in 1637 and then in 1665, took a fourteen year lease on two fields taken in from Holcombe Moor, which extended much further down the hillside than it does today. They belonged to the Kenyon family of Kenyon Clough and were described as *'le upper close and le lower close lying between le Parkditch and a close of land called le Topturfshill.'* Christopher Cronkshaw's son William bought these fields in 1678 when they were said to be *'adjoining the highway in Alden leading between Holcombe and Haslingden'* [Stake Lane]. On the 1838 Tithe Map, these fields appear as Lower Kenyon Field and Higher Kenyon Field,

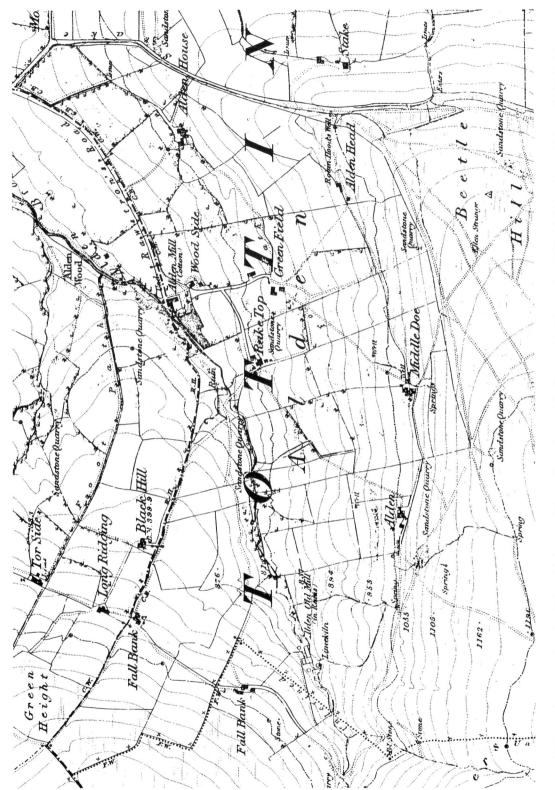

Alden in the 1840s. South of the old deer park boundary, the straight lines and right angles of the field walls recall the valley's division into 'doles' in the 17th century.

Cronkshaw Fold, the home of the Cronkshaw Family for more than 200 years, taken from the air in 1968.

recalling the name of their original owner. Much of Lower Kenyon Field is now occupied by the works associated with the gas pipeline laid in 2001.[12]

Most of the other farms in that part of Alden outside the deer park boundary also dated from the 17th or early 18th centuries. Top o' th' Rake (Alden farm now stands on the site), for example, was put up between 1631 and 1637; the long vanished Woodside farm (near Alden cottages) was standing by 1663 and Fall Bank by 1686. The land that formed Goosepits farm had been enclosed by 1662 and a lease from that year specifies that the tenant was to have liberty to dig for stones in the uppermost dole. No doubt these were used to build the house and barn shortly afterwards. Middle Doe (whose name is a corruption of Middle Dole) was of a similar date: it consisted of just a barn and fields in 1682, but a house had appeared by 1708.[13]

The land at Cronkshaw Fold was later split to create another small farm called Stake and in the early 19th century, the last of the Alden farms was built at Spring

Bank or The Township of Pilkington. The former common land that went to make up this farm amounted to just over four customary acres (about nine statute acres). We can trace part of it back to 1636 when Francis Shipplebottom and James Rothwell, both from Musbury, rented it from John Lomax. Thomas Bridge of Croichey, near Hawkshaw bought it in the mid-18th century and added another 2 acres or so to it. His descendants sold the land to Robert Pilkington of Edgworth in 1806 when it was described as *'all that part or parcel of common land lying and being in Foebank Dole in Alden upon the west part thereof.'* Robert built a house on the land and was living there with his family by 1808.[14]

Robert Pilkington is well known for his enclosure of more land in this remote corner of the valley, although on one occasion the manorial authorities thwarted his efforts to do so. In 1834, they threatened him with a fine of £100 if he did not pull down the walls he had built across *'a large extent'* of common land. His farm stood at the very northern end of the township of Tottington Lower End and was in so obscure a position that Robert managed to avoid paying any rates. He was refused poor relief during the depression of 1826 and is said to have appealed to the Government for help, saying he lived at 'The Township of Pilkington', a name by which this corner of the Alden valley is still known.[15]

LATER ENCLOSURES AND DIVISIONS

Within the old park boundaries and at Musdenhead, the process of enclosing outlying pieces of common and of subdividing existing farms continued well into the early 19th century. For example, when John Bridge of Entwistle bought Top o' th' Hillock in Musdenhead in 1738 from Benjamin and Hannah Barnes it was only a small farm with a copyhold rent of just 3d. However, at the same time John bought about two customary acres (just over four statute acres) adjoining the north-west end of the house, *'being part of a common called the Height in Musbury'* and it was agreed that this land was *'to be inclosed and fenced off from the said common as it is now marked and bounded out at the charge of the said John Bridge.'* In the next few years he added another six customary acres of common *'on Uglow'* to the farm, although this was later sold.[16]

We can clearly see the process of splitting up farms in the following example. The area of land in Musbury that Geoffrey Taylor received in 1507 had two farms on it by 1571. These were what were later to be known as Hare Clough and Higher Tan Pits farms. In 1621, the owner of Higher Tan Pits (or the Great House as it was known) divided the building into two. The east end (two bays of building) and a room called the entry chamber on the north side, parts of various outbuildings and several fields were to go to Edward Taylor and Alice Haworth, his intended wife. By the end of the 17th century, two other farms had appeared on the Higher Tan Pits land. When the owner died in 1697 his property included fields called Lower Rushie Leache and Over Rushie Leache, *'with the house and barn standing in it.'* The

Barnes Fold, one of the highest farms in Musdenhead standing at 1,150 feet above sea level. James Barnes bought the farm in 1731, but there had been people with the same surname living in Musdenhead since the late 16th century.

ruins of this farm, Rushy Leach, are still to be seen lying just within the boundary of the old deer park. The other farm lay across the valley underneath Tor and was called Further Sides.[17]

Further alterations to the Higher Tan Pits farmstead took place in the 18th and 19th centuries. By 1804, the old Great House had been divided into three and a new house built nearby, followed by a row of cottages in 1836. The Hare Clough estate also went through a process of subdivision. It supported two farms by 1762 and three by 1783. One of them was a smallholding called Nan House whose name suggests that it was intended to be used as a home for the widow of the owner of the estate when her son took over the main farm. Indeed, when Christopher Duckworth of Hare Clough died in 1783 he said that his wife Alice was to have *'either the house my son John dwells in ... or to have Nannhouse now in the possession of Joseph Barnes.'*[18]

The result of the continued process of enclosing common land and of splitting up the original landholdings into several farms was that by the time the Ordnance Survey prepared the first detailed map of the area in the 1840s, there were more than fifty farms in Musbury, Alden and Musdenhead.

NOTES

1   William Farrer (trans), *The Court Rolls of the Honor of Clitheroe* (1913), III, 406

2   Will of George Duckworth of Broughton 1815 (LRO: WCW); *Manchester Mercury* 28th November 1815; Michael McGarvie, 'The Duckworths and the building of Orchardleigh House', *Transactions of the Ancient Monuments Society,* volume 27 (1983) 119

3   Agreement 18th June 31 Eliz. I [1589] (Somerset Record Office: DD\DU/88)

4   William Farrer, *op. cit.,* p. 177. A rood fall was equivalent to a perch of land

5   Manor of Accrington records (LRO: DDHCL)

6   Ministers' accounts of the Honor of Clitheroe 1341 - *temp* Eliz I (Manchester Central Library: L1/50/36/4)

7   William Farrer, *op. cit.,* p. 406; Manor of Accrington records (LRO: DDHCL)

8   Manor of Accrington records (LRO: DDHCL Liber DG, folio 467)

9   Manor of Accrington records (LRO: DDHCL 3/109)

10   William Farrer, *op. cit.,* pp. 299, 403, 328

11   For the background to the copyhold dispute see G. H. Tupling, *The Economic History of Rossendale*, chapter v

12   Manor of Tottington records (LRO: DDHCL)

13   Manor of Tottington records (LRO: DDHCL)

14   Manor of Tottington records (LRO: DHHCL)

15   Manor of Tottington records (LRO: DDHCL)

16   Manor of Accrington records (LRO: DDHCL)

17   Manor of Accrington records (LRO: DDHCL)

18   Manor of Accrington records (LRO: DDHCL); Will of Christopher Duckworth of Hare Clough 1783 (LRO: WCW)

AT HOME AND AT WORK

WE KNOW a great deal about how the people of Musbury and Alden lived and worked in the centuries before the Industrial Revolution from information gleaned from their probate inventories and from entries in the manorial court rolls, deeds and other miscellaneous documents.

AT HOME

The first houses built after the division of the park would have been timber-framed dwellings. Many probably continued to be wholly made of wood into the 17th century, but people also used stone as a building material from an early date and there are references to places where it was quarried in the 1560s. Wills and inventories record both timber and stone for building. For example, when Ralph Haworth of Great House died in 1624 his possessions included *'a pair of crocks'* [crucks]. These huge curving timbers made the basic framework of a wooden building by being fastened together in the shape of a giant letter A which then supported the roof and walls. Ralph also had quantities of slate and stone. Thomas Duckworth of Kiln Field (died 1612) had slate worth two shillings, while his grandson (also called Thomas) stipulated in his will that his brother George was to have timber for building. When George himself died in 1665, his inventory included *'fallen timber and laths'* valued at £2. In 1676, John Haworth of Hollin Bank bequeathed *'all sheapinge timber for building'* to his daughter.

Some entries in the manorial court rolls also refer to the use of both timber and stone for building. In 1632, Edward Taylor of Musdenhead found himself with a fine of 20d after he had knocked down a building and taken away *'certaine flags or slatestone'* belonging to Henry Heap. When John Schofield of Alden leased several fields at Clough in 1649, he was to have liberty to fell trees growing on the land and use the timber to build a barn there. He could also get stones on Tor and in James Rothwell's clough for the building.[1]

The 17th century saw the rebuilding of some timber-framed houses in stone. Great House was one of the first altered in this way and the datestone from 1600 with the initials of Ralph and Alice Haworth now on a modern barn probably originates with this rebuilding. The house itself stood until 1968 and it is a great pity that it was not properly surveyed before its demolition. The house at Tor End (now a ruin) may have been a timber dwelling rebuilt in the mid or late 17th century. Local people knew it as 'The Castle' or 'The Mansion', names that may reflect the fact that it was originally a much more substantial dwelling than most of its neighbours. Of the farmhouses that still stand, Kiln Field and Higher

The so-called 'Castle' or 'Mansion' at Tor End in 1956. The house dated from the 17th century, but was altered in the 18th century and again in the 19th century. It gradually fell into ruins and was largely demolished about twenty years after the photograph was taken.

Hollin Bank may also be timber dwellings rebuilt in stone and may repay further investigation.

The rest of the houses that are still standing or lie in ruins in Musbury and Alden were stone-built in the 18th and 19th centuries. Several of them were so-called 'laithe houses', which combined a dwelling with a shippon/barn [laithe] under one roof. Usually the most prominent feature of such buildings was the large arched entry into the laithe, tall enough for a loaded hay cart or sled to pass beneath it. Where these houses stood on a hillside, the laithe was usually on the lower side of the slope to allow manure to drain away from the house. Trees farm follows this pattern, as did Burnt Hill and Trickling Water.

We can form an impression – albeit an incomplete one – of the interior of some houses from the wills and probate inventories of their occupants. In 1700 when James Duckworth of Park House drew up his will, he left various pieces of furniture to his wife and son and he mentions in which rooms in the house they stood. From these stray references we can tell that Park House was made up of one main ground floor room (the house) containing the main fireplace. Next to this were the parlour (which served mainly as an extra bedroom) and the kitchen. On the upper floor, there was a chamber (bedroom) over the parlour and two smaller rooms called the kitchen loft and the further loft. There was probably also a chamber over the house, but the will does not mention it. When John Holden of Tor End died in 1743, his neighbours who made an inventory of his goods listed

Tricking Water in 1960. The farmhouse, dated 1741, was demolished in the 1970s. The barn became a house following the sale of Great House Experimental Farm in the early 1980s.

them room by room. Again, his dwelling conformed to a simple plan of a main room with fireplace used for cooking and a parlour on the ground floor. There was also a buttery. Only one chamber is mentioned on the upper floor, but this does not mean that there were no others.

The homes of most local people in the 17th and 18th centuries would appear very sparsely furnished to our eyes. All of the surviving probate inventories, whether from well-to-do landowners or poor tenant farmers, contain a fairly standard mix of a few pieces of furniture such as tables and chairs, stools, settles, cupboards and chests, beds, ironwork used for cooking over an open fire, and pots and pans made of wood, pewter, brass and earthenware. From the second half of the 17th century, various luxury items joined these simple pieces of furniture in the inventories. Ralph Duckworth who died in 1667 had a set of silver teaspoons, as did Ann Haworth of Tor End (died 1814). Other luxury goods included clocks (long case clocks in the 18th century), books and looking glasses. In 1783, among the items at Hare Clough which Christopher Duckworth left to his wife Alice were *'the Corner cupboard with the Tea Vessels and other Implements therein Contained'* and a tea table. William Rawstron of Woodside in Alden who died in 1823 had a comfortably

furnished house whose contents included an escritoire, pictures, china, ornaments and a mahogany snap table (a three-legged table with a hinged top).[2]

The will and inventory of the Rev. John Duckworth who died in 1695 stands out from all the others. He was one of the Duckworths of Park House (although he lived at Hollin Bank) and was vicar of Haslingden for fifteen years. His bequests included a piece of *'broad'* gold, a gold ring and two silver salts to his wife Agnes; a tobacco box to Edward Hamer of Cockham; a guinea to a Mr. White for preaching his funeral sermon; 2d to everyone who attended the funeral; 20s to the poor of Musbury and 40s to the poor of Haslingden. The Haslingden share was to be spent on wheat bread that was to be given out in the porch of Haslingden church every Christmas for eight years. The Rev. Duckworth also left books to several friends and relatives. Naturally enough, they were mainly Bibles, books of sermons, catechisms and such like, but there may have been a broad hint in the bequest made to Alice, wife of Lawrence Duckworth, who was to receive a book entitled *'Ye Government of ye Tongue.'*

An inventory of Ralph Haworth's possessions at Great House following his death in 1624. It includes his farm animals, tools and household furnishings. Their total value was £136 10s 4d.

At a time when even the wealthiest Musbury farmers had only one or two beds, a couple of tables, chairs, and the odd cupboard or two, John Duckworth's home at Hollin Bank was furnished in a much more lavish style. His inventory lists five beds, four cupboards, six tables, four chests, four settles or forms, nineteen chairs and seven stools. There were stitched or embroidered cushions on some of the chairs, hangings round the beds, table-cloths and napkins in the cupboards and three Holland jugs, so called because they were made of glazed earthenware originally imported from Delft.

AT WORK

Most people in Musbury and Alden in the 16th and 17th centuries made a living by combining farming and textile making. They raised cattle, sheep, pigs and poultry. Thomas Duckworth who died at Kiln Field in 1649 was a typical farmer of his time. His livestock included four 'kine' [cows] valued at £17, three heifers (£10), four stirks (between one and two years old) and two calves (total value £8 6s 8d) and two other kine worth £6. Four oxen (£24) and four sheep (20s) completed the list of his farm animals. Other probate inventories tell us that some Musbury cattle herds included 'twinters' [cows two winters old], 'why stirks' [heifers before they had had their first calf] and sometimes a bull. James Duckworth of Park House who died in 1700 had a 'segg' [castrated bull] and John Schofield of Tor Side (died 1723) had two 'drapes' [cows which had ceased to give milk]. Many probate inventories also include dairying utensils such as churns and cheese presses as well as quantities of butter and cheese.

Both oxen and horses found a place on many farms until the early 18th century, when the use of oxen for heavy work such as ploughing began to die out. Thus, we find that in 1626, George Haworth of Hollin Bank had four oxen and two twinters worth £29 and a horse and mare valued at £10. One of the last of the Musbury farmers to use oxen was Christopher Cronkshaw of Hill End (next to Higher Tan Pits) who died in 1714. He had four oxen (£13 10s) and four steers (young castrated oxen, £11 10s). As well as providing motive power, horses also carried goods to and from the farms, and probate inventories often include harness belonging to the animals. John Schofield of Woodside in Alden (1667) had two horses 'with packsaddles & furniture', no doubt used for carrying wool and cloth in his business as a clothier. His neighbour Christopher Cronkshaw of Cronkshaw Fold who died in 1685 had two mares and packsaddles, 'wantoes & oreleis'. Wantoes were ropes used for tying down the packs, while oreleis were coverings for the loads. (The word is a corruption of 'overlay').

Only a few farms had any pigs and there were not many flocks of sheep grazing the hills. Ralph Haworth of Great House (died 1624) had one of the largest flocks of sheep with seventy-six animals, while across at Kiln Field in 1632 Ralph Duckworth had ewes, lambs and wethers valued at 51s 4d, with a further fourteen ewes and lambs worth £3 19s 4d. When Edward Taylor of Higher Tan Pits died in 1637, he bequeathed to his grandsons twenty sheep *'being hodges'* [aged from between six months old to the first shearing] which his son Gilbert was to look after for four years. One or two farmers kept poultry (usually hens, although John Schofield who died at Woodside in Alden in 1687 also had geese). George Duckworth of Kiln Field (1665) may also have kept bees since his inventory included beehives valued at 10s.

Most farmers grew cereal crops on part of their land. The earliest surviving Musbury inventory – that of Margaret Duckworth of Kiln Field who died in 1595 – includes £2 *'in corn growing'*. George Haworth of Hollin Bank (1611) had *'seed corn sown'* (55s), while Geoffrey Taylor of Higher Tan Pits who died in the same year had 20s worth of *'corn growing upon the earth.'* Henry Brooke (died 1633), a tenant of one of the farms on the Park House estate, had corn, oats and barley growing valued at £6. Quantities of arable crops and their products such as oatmeal, malt and groats (hulled and crushed grain used to feed livestock) appear on most Musbury farms from the end of the 16th century until the 1740s, when the practice of making probate inventories began to die out.

East Lancashire's wet climate and the relatively short corn growing season often made it necessary to dry the harvested grain before it could be stored. This may have taken place in a temporary kiln built in the corner of a field, but some farms had specially constructed kilns. They took the form of a lower chamber with a peat or charcoal fire from which heat rose through a perforated platform to dry the damp grain spread out in a layer. In 1750, when John Schofield bought one of the Hill End farms from the Duckworth family, he was given the right to *'dry all his grain and corn from the premises in the drying kiln standing at Parkhouse'* on the understanding that he would pay a third of the costs of its repair *'but not the new building thereof if it is ever needed.'* Some of these kilns must have been fairly substantial structures, for when Lawrence Haworth rented the Hill End farm next to Higher Tan Pits in 1790, its buildings included *'a house anciently a kiln.'*[3]

Farmers kept their land in good heart by spreading farmyard manure or *'worthing'*, quantities of which appear in several inventories. Field names such as 'marled earth' and 'limed earth' also suggest they used marl and lime. Indeed, in 1609 when John Duckworth transferred part of the Park House estate to trustees, Richard Entwistle (who had acquired an interest in the land) claimed the right to dig marl on it.[4] Lime was important for sweetening the acid soil especially on the high farms in Musdenhead where at least one property was described in the late 17th century as having *'very Barren and Moorish lands.'*[5] Several 18th century leases made strict provisions about the use of lime. In 1748, for instance, Richard Holden agreed to spread ten loads of lime on Trees farm every year for seven years. Another lease of the same farm in 1763 said that the lime was to be spread *'in a husbandmanlike manner.'* John Kay, the owner of Rushy Leach farm in 1787, agreed to apply twelve loads of lime to the land in the first year of a lease to the new tenant

Aprill 10th 1723

A true and perfect Inventory of all the goods and Chat=
=tels and Substanse of John Scholfield of Torr side deceased

	£ s d
Imprimis in purse and Apparell	72-00-00
Item in two Cowes & two Calves	07-10-00
Item two barren Cowes	06-10-00
Item two drapes	05-00-00
Item two Cows and two Hefers	12-00-00
Item three Twinters	06-06-00
Item three Horses with furniture	12-00-00
Item in Meal and Malt & Wheat	17-00-00
Item in Corne and Hay	03-00-00
Item in Wollen Cloath	24-00-00
Item in Wool and Yarn	08-00-00
Item in three beds and beding	05-10-00
Item in two pair of Loomes & warpin woues	02-00-00
Item in ton Backs	01-05-00
Item in four Arkes	02-00-00
Item in dust and grund meal	00-14-00
Item in two Chests & table in Chambere	00-10-00
Item in Beef Beacon Butter & Cheese	00-18-00
Item one Clock and Case	02-18-00
Item one one table & Cupboard & Chest in house	01-08-00
Item in pewter & brass and pans	02-06-08
Item in griddo & Thrown vessells boards & troncheres	01-01-00
Item in Chairs Cushions and stools	00-09-00
Item in earthen vessels	00-06-08
Item in one Churn briggs tonges & Chafing dish	00-08-00
Item one Ax wimbles Chizells & piniors	00-06-00
Item in Carts wheels and slods	01-10-00
Item one plow harrows and swingletrees	01-05-00
Item in Spades forks shools soales	00-07-00
Item one Laddor and a Crost	00-03-06
Item one grinding stone	00-02-06
Item in Wheels Cards and meat board	00-12-06
Item in Smothing irns heaters & other Husloments	01-00-00

Apprised by us
Thomas Durkworth
James Taylor
Richard Scoffield

£ 67
Sum totall-200-06-08

One of the last probate inventories from Musbury and Alden. John Schofield lived at Tor
Side farm and died in 1723. His stock of 'Wollen Cloath' worth £24 was one of his most
valuable possessions.

Christopher Duckworth, but in return, Duckworth was '*not to plough above one field in one year. And not to have liberty to sell fodder off after the manner of the last tenant at his quitting the place and not to sell or dispose of any manure, tillage or ashes arising from the said premises.*' The duty of spreading lime at Hill End (near Higher Tan Pits) was shared between landlord and tenant in 1790, while at Further Sides in the same year John Ramsbottom, the landlord, agree to pay 9d per load for 100 horse loads or '*windles*' of lime for the farm.

THE HARVEST OF THE HILLS

The farmers of Musbury and Alden supplemented the resources of their landholdings by exploiting the surrounding moorlands. Alden farms had access to Holcombe Moor; Great House, Tor End and Hollin Bank had rights on Tor; the farms on the north side of Musbury such as Hare Clough, Higher Tan Pits, Kiln Field and Park House shared Musbury Heights [Gorse Edge]; and Musdenhead farms used Uglow [Hoglowe] Moor and the stretch of moor over to Broadhead. These moorland areas had a variety of uses.

Some farmers had the right to graze horses, cattle or sheep on the moors but, to ensure that they were not overgrazed, there were agreements stating when and in what numbers animals could be taken on to them. In 1554, for example, when Joan Haworth received a house and land, part of Hollin Bank, she also was given '*owtlawse for her beasts upon the Torre yearly between Martinmas* [11th November] *and 25th March.*'[6] Another part of the Hollin Bank property consisting of a barn and several fields passed from George Haworth to his son John in 1593 and brought with it '*two beastes gates*' on Tor. A beast gate was the right to graze one horned animal. In the second half of the 17th century, the tenant of Hare Clough had the right to pasture one horse a year on the Height from 1st May to the feast of St. Michael [29th September]. Of course, there were times when the agreements about the pasturing of animals on the moors were broken. In 1693, John and Nicholas Rawstorne of Alden were fined 6d each at the manorial court for putting cattle, sheep and other animals on Holcombe Moor '*contrary to the stint*'. The stint was the number of animals that farmers with rights on the common were allowed to graze there.

Perhaps the second most important use of the moors was the exercise of the right of turbary, which meant cutting peat to use as fuel and digging turf and sods for a variety of purposes such as repairing field banks. As with the grazing of animals, turbary was limited in various ways. In 1682, for example, when Richard Gryme took over Black Hill farm he acquired the right of '*Two dayes delfe of Turfes*' each year. Similarly, in 1734, John Butterworth took a ten year lease of one of the Hill End farms and could dig peat but only for one day a year. The owners or occupiers of some farms were restricted to digging peat in particular areas known as turf rooms. In 1650, a lease of Clough farm in Alden brought with it '*liberty to get and dig turfs in the usual turf rooms on the Torr height in any place whatsoever, 8 cart or waine loads per year.'* An unusual agreement about turbary appears in a lease of Burnt Hill in 1687 when the landlord Robert Roscoe of Bolton gave his tenant Thomas Duckworth the right to sell turf and peat in return for an annual rent of £6 and for taking twelve horse loads of turf to Bolton every year for sixteen years.

People treated turf rooms as part of their farms and handed them on from generation to generation in the same way. When Richard Cronkshaw who lived at Rake Foot made his will in 1618, he left to his son William *'one mosse rowme as the same is sett forth upon the lands of John Hargraves sonne of Henry and all my right therein saveinge that ... Ellen my wife shall have sufficient turbarie dureinge her life.'* As late as 1814, John Barnes of Barnes Fold granted his wife a *'Right and privilege to get Turf on Musdenhead height and Liberty of a Road to Lead and Room to Lay the same near the ... Dwelling house.'*

The commons were also an important source of stone, although farmers could also dig stone on their own land, and small abandoned quarries like that behind Further Sides farm are still prominent features in the landscape. Leases of various farms often contained clauses giving the tenants the right to get stone on the commons. In 1619, for instance, John Robert of Musdenhead acquired a piece of land in *'Musden and Ugden'* on the south side of the Height which brought with it a right of way and *'liberty to dig and get stones in le height at the side of the way for the necessary uses of the said premises.'* Similarly, when Ralph Haworth rented out Trickling Water farm to Francis Shipplebottom in 1636, he gave his new tenant the right to get

A landscape of stone. Local people quarried stone in Musbury and Alden to build their houses, barns and shippons and to enclose their fields with strong walls. This view from Hare Clough in 1946 clearly shows the old stone pit above Further Sides farm.

stone on his part of Tor. Middle Doe farm included part of the 'stonedelves' in the common and waste in Alden in 1722, while in 1747 when James Taylor bought the so-called 'Old House' at Tor End it brought with it the right to get both turf and stone on Tor.

One of the Duckworth documents in Somerset also refers to quarrying stone on Gorse Edge. It is an agreement made in December 1560 by Ralph Duckworth, William Cronkshaw, Richard Duckworth and John Cronkshaw, which states that they had divided Gorse Edge among themselves. Lying within several of the shares or doles were *'a certaine Well springe and stone pitt'*. The four men agreed that they could all have access to the spring *'to wash, fetch water & water bese and Cattelle'* and that they could all go to the stone pit to get stone. Moreover, they all had the right to *'search breck soyle & Make stone pitts & such stone pitts so made everye one of them to be free to get up stones to their owne uses.'* [7]

TEXTILES

Most families in Musbury and Alden in the 16th, 17th and 18th centuries were involved in the production of cloth in one way or another and many probate inventories list yarn or cloth making equipment. To take a typical example, Jeffrey Taylor who died in 1624 left a pair of looms *'with other things thereunto belonging'* valued at 13s 4d; spinning wheels and cards; and wool and woollen yarn worth £14. These last two items were worth almost the same as all his cattle and two horses. Many people, such as John Holden of Tor End who died in 1674, had combs and a combstock, used for preparing long staple wool ready for it to be spun into worsted yarn. Several early 18th century inventories also contain 'warping woughs', frames on which threads were arranged to create warps.

Occasionally the people who drew up an inventory specified particular types of cloth. Ralph Duckworth who died in 1667 had canvas bocking worth 13s 4d, while Christopher Cronkshaw of Cronkshaw Fold (died 1685) had five yards of dyed kersey valued at 15s. However, neither had any textile making equipment in their inventories so they may have bought the cloth from someone else. When John Rothwell of Musbury died in 1743 (possibly at Hollin Bank), he had one piece [a length of cloth] *'i'th' looms'* and another *'at milling.'* In this instance, the second length of cloth was away being finished at a nearby fulling mill. At this date, the nearest fulling mill was at Ravenshore.

Gradually, people started to describe themselves and their neighbours as textile workers in some way or other rather than just farmers or husbandmen. John Fielden who was at Clough farm in 1696 was said to be a 'cloth maker', while the people who made a list of Henry Taylor's goods in May 1711 gave his occupation as 'woollen webster,' even though he also had cows, horses and sheep, ploughs, harrows and other farming implements. Richard Ashworth and John Rothwell, the new tenants of Higher and Lower Hollin Bank in 1733, were both described as websters, while John and George Haworth who rented Lower Houses in 1745 were woollen weavers. The Musbury and Alden textile workers also included clothiers and chapmen. John Schofield of Woodside in Alden was one of the first people in the district who made a living as a clothier, a man who bought raw wool and put it out to spinners and weavers as well as making cloth himself. When he died in 1667 he farmed quite a large area of Alden and at Clough farm and had the usual mix of farm stock along with two pairs of looms *'with other appurtenances'* valued at £1 6s 8d. The manorial records also identify Edmund Duckworth who bought Trees farm in 1722 as a clothier, as was Henry Taylor, the purchaser of Charity farm in 1735. Chapmen (like Lawrence Rawstron at Park House in 1744 and John Barnes at Barnes Fold in 1764) brought supplies of wool and yarn to spinners and weavers and then helped them to sell their finished lengths of cloth.

The tasks of spinning and weaving usually took place in one of the rooms in the farmhouse. John Rothwell's 1743 inventory lists the contents of his dwelling room by room and shows that his looms were in the 'house', the main downstairs room. At Tor End where John Holden died in 1744, the looms were in one of the upstairs chambers. A description of one of the Hill End farms, near Park House in 1744 mentions a 'loom house', suggesting that here there was a separate workshop housing the handlooms.

TRADES AND CRAFTS

Some people combined farming and cloth making with some trade or craft. Christopher Cronkshaw of Musbury who died in 1692 was a carpenter and he bequeathed a *'Bag of Carpenter Work Tooles'* to John Haworth. Another member of the Cronkshaw family, William, who died at Rake Foot in 1711, was a shoemaker, while Ralph Rishton who mortgaged one of the Musdenhead farms at Michaelmas 1710 was a tailor.

Several members of the Duckworth family made their living by tanning leather. It seems that their original tan-pits were on the site now occupied by Barlow Terrace and it was probably here that the *'old bark house'* stood which is mentioned in a description of the Park House estate in 1750. This building would have stored strips of oak bark, an important ingredient in the tanning process. Hides had to be soaked for many months in deep pits containing a liquor that included ground up oak bark. Before they reached this stage, however, they had been scraped several times and soaked in vats of limewater and water mixed with chicken or dog dung. It was hard work and very smelly. In 1707, Lawrence Duckworth bought one of the farms further up the valley and within a few years had built a new set of tan-pits there. In doing so, he gave the farm a new name – Higher Tan Pits – by which it is still known.

The Duckworths established a third tan-yard in the second half of the 18th century not far from the old one belonging to Park House. John Duckworth (who was living at Hollin Bank) acquired a small field called Little Holme from Lawrence Duckworth of Park House in 1761. It adjoined Blind Lane (apparently an old name for Tanner Bank Lane). He built a bark house on it and added a dwelling house in 1780. This tan-yard was still in existence in 1809, but William and Ralph Turner cleared it to make way for part of Middle Mill when they bought the property in 1835.[8]

NOTES

[1] Manor of Accrington records (LRO: DDHCL 3/114 and 3/132)
[2] William Rawstron's inventory is reproduced in Patrick Stephens and Richard Hawkin, *Historical Notices of Helmshore and Musbury, Part VI,* (1929), pp. 89 - 90
[3] R. W. Brunskill, *Traditional Farm Buildings of Britain,* (1982), p. 94; Manor of Accrington records (LRO: DDHCL Liber E, folio 178; Liber T, folio 315)
[4] Manor of Accrington records (LRO: DDHCL 3/92)
[5] Petition of Henry Haworth of Musbury, 10th December 1679 (NA: PL6/33, no. 137)
[6] William Farrer (trans), *The Court Rolls of the Honor of Clitheroe,* III, p. 178
[7] Agreement dated 3rd December 3 Eliz. I [1560] (Somerset Record Office: DD\DU/88)
[8] The tan-yard is marked on the map of the new turnpike road from Brandlesome to Blackburn, 1809 (LRO: PDS/13)

THE INDUSTRIAL AGE

THE PACE OF LIFE began to quicken in the two valleys as the 18th century drew to a close. The Musbury and Alden brooks provided supplies of water for several small mills, which made their appearance in the twenty years or so either side of 1800. The first mill was built in 1790 in a corner of the Park House estate at Tan Pits. In June of that year, Lawrence Duckworth leased to Robert Haworth for eleven years *'all that working machine or carding engines with the new erected building, the water works and other utensils … and liberty for enlargement of the dams or lodge … at Lower Parkhouse.'* This little mill ran for almost two hundred years, although James Barlow and Sons rebuilt it and renamed it Albert Mill in 1886.

Other water-powered mills soon joined the Park House carding engine. Midge Hole Mill at the foot of the Alden valley dated from about 1794, Hare Clough Mill from 1797 and the original Sunnybank Mill from 1798. Foundry Mill (just upstream from Midge Hole) was built between 1798 and 1800, Slidings Mill in 1801 and Lower Sunnybank Mill sometime before 1809. By the early 1830s, the list of mills in the two valleys also included Alden bleach-works at the very head of the valley, Higher and Lower Alden Mills, Clough Mill, Carrs Mill, and Tan Pits dye-works (later Barlow's mill).

To begin with, all of the mills were used either for carding wool or for fulling and finishing woollen cloth, but the change to cotton began shortly after 1800. In 1806, for instance, when Thomas Worsick and James Schofield took a seven-year lease on Slidings Mill they converted it to cotton spinning.[2] The first purpose-built cotton factory in either Musbury or Alden was Higher Alden Mill. It stood near the little bridge over Alden brook just below Top o' th' Rake (now Alden farm) and was built in about 1810 by the Rawstron family who owned Black Hill, Woodside and Top o' th' Rake. It must have been of modest dimensions for a note in an 1837 valuation gives its total power as just 2½ horsepower.[3] Water taken out of the brook a short distance upstream made its way to the mill in a goit along the hillside which survives as a weed-choked channel.

The Rawstrons rented out this mill to a succession of small manufacturers, but perhaps when they realised that fortunes could be made in the cotton industry they decided to build themselves a mill a little downstream in the 1820s. It was on a larger scale and had a reservoir to ensure a more reliable source of water. Its construction may have led to the demise of the higher mill, which had fallen into ruin by the time of the 1844 Ordnance Survey map.

Like Higher Alden Mill, two other mills on the Alden brook had relatively short lives. Once Robert Pilkington had established himself at Spring Bank, he built a small bleach-works on land next to the brook at the bottom of one of his fields. He

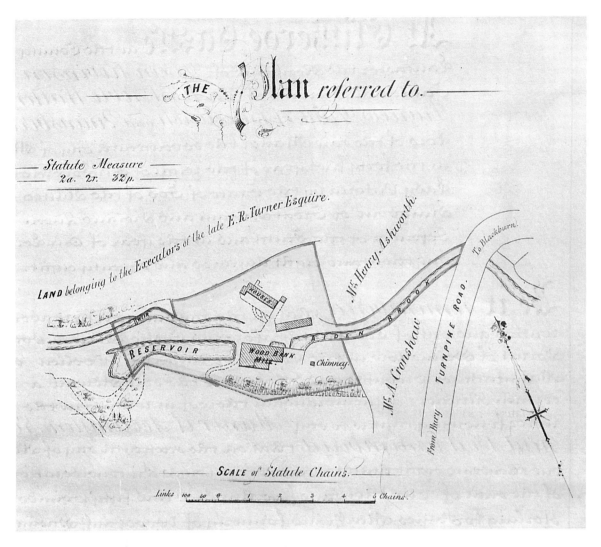

THE Plan _referred to._

Statute Measure
2a. 2r. 32p.

Land belonging to the Executors of the late E.R.Turner Esquire.

Mr Henry Ashworth.

To Blackburn.

WEIR

RESERVOIR

HOUSES

WOOD BANK MILL

Chimney

AIDEN BROOK

Mr A. Cronshaw.

From Bury TURNPIKE ROAD.

SCALE of Statute Chains.

Links 100 50 0 1 2 3 4 5 Chains.

Midge Hole or Wood Bank Mill in 1878 when it was bought by William John Porritt.
He demolished the mill and nearby houses and used the stone to build Wood Bank
Cottages and homes for his senior staff.
[_Source: Lancashire Record Office DDHLC Liber CT_]

may have run the works himself for a time, but later leased them to other people
such as Anthony Hartley and Abraham Brown who were there in 1833. The
building is said to have burnt down and the first edition six-inch Ordnance Survey
map shows the buildings in ruins, although the outline of the walls survive to this
day.[4]

Further downstream, almost at Sunnybank, stood Clough Mill. You reach its site
by taking the path through the iron gate at the side of the former Porritt stables.
Once through a small wooded area you can see a few pieces of masonry next to the

brook and it was here the mill stood. Like the bleach-works, we do not know exactly when it was built, although it probably dated from the 1820s. It belonged to James Duckworth of Clough who appears as a cotton spinner and manufacturer in a trade directory of 1828. The mill appears on a map of 1833 but all standing trace of it had disappeared ten years later.[5]

The owners of most of the early 19th century mills employed only a handful of workers. At Midge Hole Mill, for example, James Ashworth and his son-in-law James Markland had a workforce of just six people in 1861, while at the original Sunnybank Mill James Barlow employed twelve. Twenty-six people worked for John Tattersall at the old Tan Pits Mill in the same year. John Cronkshaw, a member of the Cronkshaw Fold family, ran Hare Clough Mill for a time in the late 1840s and early 1850s. In 1848,

The ruins of Robert Pilkington's bleach-works at the head of Alden. The trees on the skyline mark the site of Robert's farm, the Township of Pilkington.

he approached the Bolton Poor Law Guardians saying that he would take five orphan children from the workhouse and employ them in his mill or house. He agreed to clothe and look after them in his home but said:

> He should not be obliged to retain them for any specified period, nor would he require that the children should be required to remain with him longer than they were satisfied with his behaviour towards them.[6]

The 1851 census returns show that he had four teenaged girls living with his family. Three were born in Bolton, the other in Manchester and all were working as cotton piecers. James Barlow and Ashworth and Markland may also have employed children from the workhouse: in the 1861 census both had teenaged boys and girls from Liverpool living in their households, some of whom were cotton piecers.[7]

A decided contrast to these small concerns were the mills run by the Turner family, two of which stood within Musbury township. The family moved into the district in 1789 when they built Helmshore Mill (now Higher Mill) and by the early 19th century, they owned one of the largest firms in the woollen trade. They employed weavers in the vicinity and as far afield as Rochdale to produce cloth, which they then brought to Helmshore for fulling and finishing.

The Turners began to expand their industrial empire in 1818 when they took a 31-year lease on the 1790 carding mill at Tan Pits. In the next few years, the partnership of James and Edward Turner and then of James's sons William and Ralph bought small pieces of land near the carding mill from both the owner of the Park House estate and the owner of the adjoining Hollin Bank property. In 1822, for instance, they paid £114 for a piece of land on which stood four cottages and a reservoir and acquired the right to divert the stream in the Cote Meadow which belonged to Hollin Bank. The reservoir was at the bottom of Tanner Bank Lane, while James Barlow and Sons Ltd later used the cottages as offices. They survive as houses. In the following year, James and Edward Turner paid a further £120 for another plot on the adjoining property on which they built a dye-works.[8]

Once they had completed the dye-works, the Turners turned their attention to manufacturing cloth using the newly developed power loom. They bought another part of the Hollin Bank estate fronting the turnpike road from Blackburn to Bury (now Holcombe Road) and began to erect a power loom factory ninety-six yards long and five storeys high. By December 1823, the new building was nearly complete but a severe storm almost totally destroyed it.[9] Work recommenced and soon a seven-storeyed building stood towering over the road and nearby cottages.

William Turner, the Helmshore woollen manufacturer.
Two of his mills (Middle Mill and Tan Pits dye-works) stood within
Musbury township and he also owned Clough and Tor End farms.

Bad luck was to continue to dog Middle Mill (as it was called) for several years. It had not been long set to work when rioters attacked it in April 1826, smashing all 106 looms in the building and causing an estimated £1,651 worth of damage. Disaster struck again in 1828. By this date, several other buildings had been added to the mill forming a square, with the power loom factory across its north end. On the west side stood a four-storey building comprising a boiler house on the ground floor and warehouse and storerooms above. A fire broke out in this building in November 1828. The *Bolton Chronicle* gave this account of the fire:

> The devouring element was most rapid in its work of destruction, and the protection of any part of the building and its contents was seen to be beyond human control. In little more than an hour from the first discovery of the fire the whole of the factory was reduced to ashes. It soon became obvious that the exertions of the immense crowd which had assembled could only be made available in protecting the power loom factory, which for some time appeared to be falling a sacrifice to the flames. By means of about five hundred small tin vessels a continuous stream of water was kept falling down that side of the factory wall which was connected with the flaming edifice; and though all the mill doors on that side were turned to ashes and all the windows destroyed the perilous and praiseworthy exertions of those who had the direction of the assistance, saved the factory and with it property to the amount, it is supposed, of £40,000.

During the fire, Henry Rothwell, a loom overlooker, died after falling through a trapdoor over the engine house. He left a wife and eight children.[10]

Middle Mill foreshadowed the larger mills that appeared in Musbury and Alden in the second half of the 19th century. John Tattersall built the first of these. In about 1860, he set up in business as a cotton hard waste manufacturer in the old carding mill at Tan Pits. Four years later, he paid £1,490 2s for a piece of land just to the north of the reservoir and built a new mill, which he called Park Mill. Tattersall's business failed in 1879 and his mill passed to Henry Worsley, Benjamin Haworth and Thomas Law who extended it in 1893. This three-storeyed brick building is still a prominent feature of Holcombe Road. It originally housed about seventy looms on the ground floor with carding and spinning above, but the first use to which it was put had nothing to do with cloth making at all. In December 1893, the newly completed mill was the venue for Helmshore Conservative Club's tea and dance. About 100 guests sat down to the meal, followed by dancing accompanied by Helmshore Brass Band.[11]

A couple of years after the completion of Park Mill, changes began at Sunnybank that were to have a profound effect on the subsequent history of Alden, Musbury and Helmshore as a whole. Joseph Porritt, formerly senior partner in the firm of Porritt Brothers and Austin at Stubbins Vale, was on the look out for a site to build a new mill. He had withdrawn from the partnership in 1858 and had set up business with his sons in Ramsbottom. The new firm (Joseph Porritt and Sons) had run into problems at the Ramsbottom mill because effluent from the wool cleansing and fulling departments had found its way into the River Irwell.

They decided to try to make a fresh start on a new site where they could build settling tanks to deal with the waste in a proper fashion.

The Porritts had heard that Foundry Mill was for sale and soon agreed to buy it. At the same time, they began negotiating with James Barlow to buy his woollen and cotton mills at Sunnybank, mainly to secure water rights along the Alden brook. Barlow is said to have had asked for a large sum of money because he knew that without the Sunnybank estate the Porritts' project would fail. Following some hard bargaining, Barlow received £4,000 for his property and moved his business to the dye-works at Tan Pits.[12]

Joseph Porritt and his sons set about building a new four-storey mill on the site of Foundry Mill. It was completed in June 1867 when *'upwards of eighty persons'* were treated to a dinner at the White Horse.[13] Joseph Porritt died in the following year leaving his son William John to shoulder responsibility for the business. He built himself a large house on the hillside above the mill and began to add rows of cottages for his workpeople, partly reusing stone from the old Sunnybank, Foundry and Midge Hole Mills.[14] There is an 1856 datestone with the initials of James and Rachel Barlow incorporated into the rear wall of 5, Sunnybank Cottages. For a time, Porritt also used part of the original Sunnybank Mill as a wool warehouse. He completed his acquisition of the mills along the Alden brook with the purchase of Alden Mill in 1875.[15]

While these changes were taking place at Sunnybank, the mills that had belonged to William Turner were also beginning a new chapter in their history. Following Turner's death in 1852, Middle Mill may have stood empty for a while as dozens of people left the village to find work elsewhere. By 1861, however, Turner's trustees had been able to find a tenant. John Haworth, a fulling miller at Cams Mill, had gone into partnership with his son Abraham as cotton hard waste spinners and manufacturers and they moved into Middle Mill. The difficult years of the Cotton Famine may have wrecked their business for they went bankrupt in 1866.[16]

William John Porritt, for many years the driving force behind the success of Joseph Porritt and Sons. He was said to have demanded 'something better than best' from both himself and his workpeople and personally oversaw all the extensions and improvements to Sunnybank Mill. By the time of his death in 1896, he had also bought most of the farms in both Alden and Musbury.

Their successors at Middle Mill were the brothers John and Robert Ashworth who were grocers and drapers by trade. In the late 1850s, they had gained a foothold in the cotton trade by taking over Ravenshore Mill and by 1861, they were employing one hundred people. They added Middle Mill to their business in the late 1860s and by 1871, they had been able to buy it and had a workforce of two hundred people at their two mills. John Ashworth died in 1877 and Robert moved to Newchurch and ran a mill at Lumb, although he retained an interest in the Helmshore partnership. Middle Mill continued under the eye of Betty, John Ashworth's widow. She must have been a determined character for, despite the loss of her husband, daughter and son within a short space of time, she bought Middle Mill when her brother-in-law sold the partnership's property in 1886.[17] Soon after, she set about building a new weaving shed to house 580 looms and in 1888 took down the top two storeys of Turner's seven-storeyed mill and used the stone to build the houses known as 'The Grandstand' on Holcombe Road. In the meantime, she leased the mill to a new limited company.[18]

A group of men from Helmshore and Haslingden set up the Middle Mill Manufacturing Company in 1887. They nearly all worked in the cotton trade, except for the landlords of the White Horse, Helmshore and the Dyers Arms, Haslingden. Their company ran the mill for nearly ten years, although things did not always go smoothly between the directors and their employees. Matters came to a head in May 1889 when the weavers became dissatisfied with the money they received for the lengths of cloth they had woven and suspected that the company was defrauding them in some way. They asked a factory inspector to call to look into the matter. He checked the lengths of cloth using the yardstick belonging to the firm. All seemed to be in order until he decided to measure the yardstick itself. He found that it was 37½ inches in length, although it was marked as only 36 inches. The company faced prosecution for the fraud, but eventually William Bentley, the manager, agreed to publish a statement in which he confessed to using a falsely marked measure and the case was dropped.[19]

Another clash with the manager took place a few weeks later when he posted a notice saying there had been complaints about the quality of the cloth sent to Manchester and asked the weavers to do better. They countered by saying that they could not weave better cloth without better weft and went on strike for a fortnight. The question of back pay for the cloth that had been short-measured was not settled until the end of the year. Relations between some of the board of directors were also not very friendly and led to a slander case being prosecuted at the Manchester Assizes shortly before the company was wound up in 1896. Rawstron Whittaker, a fulling miller at Higher Mill, was also a director of the Middle Mill Company and he and his brothers did a lot of carrying for the mill, but did not press for payment of their account until eventually it stood at £723. At a dinner in January 1896, Thomas Banks, another shareholder, was alleged to have said that the Whittakers were 'nothing but thieves and rogues' and that the company did not owe them any money. The jury found for the plaintiff and awarded him one farthing damages.[20]

The second of William Turner's Musbury mills - the Tan Pits dye-works - was sold in 1862 to James Rothwell and George Larter who were in partnership as cotton spinners at Hare Clough Mill. It is a strange irony that Larter should become owner of the dye-works since in 1836 he had been brought from his native Suffolk to work in Turner's mills under a Government migration scheme. Rothwell and Larter dissolved their partnership in 1862 and shortly afterwards they sold the mill to William Bentley who made printed carpets. In 1867, he leased it for ten years to James and John Barlow who transferred their business from Alden and renamed the dye-works Sunnybank Mill. James Barlow bought the mill in 1874 and his descendants ran it almost until its closure. Since it stood partly over Musbury Brook, the mill suffered a great deal of damage during a thunderstorm in July 1881 when flood waters washed some of the machinery into the River Ogden. In 1893, the Barlows extended the mill by adding a weaving shed for 116 looms.[21]

The older mills in Musbury were to disappear in the second half of the 19th century. With the building of turnpike roads and of the railway, the focus of industry and housing switched from the outlying valleys like Musbury and Alden to the new village that was growing up in Helmshore. In order to survive the fact that they were now somewhat out on a limb, the three mills in the upper part of Musbury changed from fulling woollen cloth to cotton hard waste spinning and weaving. Their raw material was a by-product of mule spinning and consisted of tubes of hardened cotton yarn ('cop bottoms') formed when the spindles were coated with starch paste before spinning began. Cop bottoms were broken down in machines called devils, the fibres carded and re-spun and the yarn used to weave coarse sheetings and twills. Often a batch of cop bottoms would contain pieces of scrap metal, which caused a spark when struck by the teeth of the devils, and fires were a common occurrence in cotton hard waste mills. Fire played a part in the demise of all three of the mills in the upper Musbury valley.

Hare Clough Mill was the first to go in July 1873. Its owner James Rothwell was taking advantage of a plentiful supply of water to run the devils through the night. About one o' clock in the morning a spark from some object in the waste set fire to the cotton. Rothwell extinguished it and went outside for a short time. The fire flared up again and set the mill alight. Before long, the whole building was ablaze and was soon completely destroyed. It was never rebuilt, but its lodge provided a welcome place for village children to cool off on hot days until it was drained in 1988.[22]

Slidings Mill met a similar fate in 1878 when it was in the hands of John Firth whose wife was the granddaughter of Thomas Worsick who had leased the mill in 1806.[23] The mill had closed for the Whitsuntide holidays, but early one morning, John Firth was roused from his bed by a loud crackling noise. When he looked out of his window, he saw the three-storeyed section of the mill engulfed in flames. It

The boiler house and engine house of the mill at Tan Pits, pictured in the 1960s when it had been the home of James Barlow and Sons for almost one hundred years. In the foreground is the site of Ashworth Street and the corner of Albert Mill is just visible on the right

was soon reduced to ashes, although the breaking-up room, mixing room, engine and boiler house, and water wheel were saved by breaching the embankment of the lodge (which was level with the top storey) and allowing the water to run into the mill. Firth never rebuilt the main part of the mill, but he continued to use the remaining buildings for a short time. He emigrated to Australia in the 1880s and the mill fell into ruins. We can still see the embankment of its lodge next to the brook, opposite the site of Longfield House. John Firth's son Thomas returned to Musbury in June 1904. His wife wrote in her diary:

> To Musbury to see Jim Barlow. He took us a long walk all round Tom's home. We went inside and Tom shed a tear at the old recollections. We walked past the old cotton mill, which has fallen down, and along one side of the Tor... It is a very curious, old-fashioned place. Everything looked nice and green.[24]

Carrs Mill stood on land in a bend of Musbury Brook at the end of Carr Lane cottages. It was fairly small, consisting of a three-storeyed main building with a warehouse and cottage adjoining. Water to power the mill came from the brook just below Slidings Mill and fed into a lodge behind the cottages. The water wheel was later replaced by a turbine, which itself made way for a small steam engine in the early 1880s.[25] Thomas Worsick built the mill between 1823 and 1826, along with a farmhouse and adjacent cottages. (Two more cottages were added in 1841).[26] Like Slidings Mill, Carrs passed from the Worsicks to John Firth and then to William John Porritt. By 1890, the mill's tenants were Abraham and James Hindle, cotton hard waste dealers and manufacturers from Haslingden. On 1st October of that year a fire caused by a spark in a breaking-up machine destroyed much of the stock of raw material and badly damaged the building, whose roof fell in. Abraham Hindle struggled to save the mill and in doing so inhaled a great deal of smoke which affected his lungs. This, coupled with the shock of the financial loss because the mill was uninsured, brought on his death a few days after the fire.[27] The mill then stood disused until 1920 when its masonry went to build the new road across the fields from Carr Lane to Tan Pits.

HANDLOOM WEAVING

Handloom weaving did not die out with the introduction of the power loom, but lingered on until the 1870s. In the 1851 census, there were fifteen handloom weavers in Musbury and Alden. They included Joseph Trickett and his son and daughter, William and Betty, at Higher Hollin Bank; Betty and Ann Rothwell at Trees; Henry Haworth at Rushy Leach; Thomas Bentley at Clough and Miles Lonsdale in Alden (at either Cronkshaw Fold or Old Rocks, near the White Horse). Miles was still weaving by hand in 1861 when he was 74 years old, as was 60-year-old Lawrence Cowpe at Park House. John Mort, the Porritts' gamekeeper, told historian Dr. G.H. Tupling in 1920 that he could remember a Mrs. Entwistle who

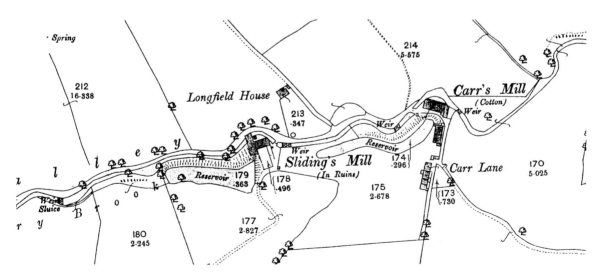

Carrs Mill at Carr Lane in 1891, with the ruins of Slidings Mill a short way upstream.

lived at Top o' th' Hillock weaving blue and white gingham handkerchiefs on her handloom in the late 1860s, using warp and weft obtained from Edgworth.[28] When the Porritt family built their mill at Sunnybank, they brought some of their workpeople from Ramsbottom. They included a few woollen handloom weavers, the last of whom seems to have been 65-year-old Richard Bentley who was living at Wood Bank at the time of the 1871 census.

We have already seen that, apart from a possible exception at Hill End, there do not appear to have been any purpose-built loom shops for handloom weaving in the two valleys. Instead, weavers used a room in their house. This was certainly the case at Woodside in Alden where William Rawstron had '*1 pare of Cotton looms*' worth 15s in his cellar in 1823.[29] Cellar loom shops were quite common since their damp atmosphere helped to prevent threads from breaking.

FARMING

By the beginning of the 19th century, there were some fifty farms in Musbury and Alden, many of which extended to just a few acres. The tenants of Nan House, which stood next to the old deer park boundary near Rushy Leach, for instance, told the census enumerators in 1861 and 1871 that they farmed just three acres. Some of the other farms were much larger, although they included areas of rough pasture as in the case of Burnt Hill where Richard Haworth was farming 95 acres in 1881. Just over the hill in Alden, William Gaskell, the tenant at Great House, had 70 acres. This included land from its neighbour Halliwells whose farmhouse the Porritts demolished in the 1870s. Several other farms had disappeared by the end of the 19th century. They included Top o' th' Bent which stood just under the slopes of Tor, above Tor End; Top of Meadow (at the head of Musbury, not far from Causeway End), Top of Great Meadow (near Bailiffs Rake) and Nan House.

Most farmers raised dairy cattle, producing milk and butter for neighbouring towns and villages. In the early 1800s, traditional Lancashire Longhorns still found a place on most farms, but by the mid-19th century, Shorthorns had largely replaced them. In October 1874, for instance, Richard Taylor at Great House sold twenty-three head of short-horned cattle '*including present and early calvers and numerous useful dairy cows, heifers and promising stirks of choice colour and breed.*' Farm stock also included poultry (not just hens, but also geese and turkeys at Hill End and Tor End in the 1880s) and pigs. Some farms had flocks of sheep too. The stock that Henry Hargreaves sold at Fall Bank farm in February 1860, for example, included ten lonk ewes in lamb. Richard Haworth of Great House had seventy half bred and lonk sheep for breeding purposes and a Leicester ram in 1874, while a couple of years later John Tattersall had fifty sheep, forty fat lambs, five fat shearlings and four fat ewes at Tan Pits.

As the 19th century wore on, local farmers gave up growing cereal crops, especially after the construction of the railways, which made it easier to bring in

One of the many farm sale notices which appeared in local newspapers in the 19th century. In this example dating from 1869, Thomas Pilkington offers for sale his stock at Middle Doe in Alden (called Middle Dover in the advertisement).

grain from elsewhere. In May 1844, the Tithe Commissioners noted that in Musbury 'Corn is only grown in very small patches after Potatoes' and William Turner told the Commission that he thought there was no more than four customary acres (just over eight statute acres) of arable land in the township.[30] The Tithe Map and schedule for that part of Alden which was in Tottington Higher End shows that all the land there was either meadow or pasture with no arable at all.

A report on Lancashire farming in 1849 said that:

In the mountainous district on the east side of the county, from Blackburn and Burnley in the north, to Bolton, Bury and Rochdale in the south … the occupiers of land … can scarcely be considered farmers: many of them being persons engaged in some way or other with the mining, manufacturing, or some other of the multifarious occupations of the district.[31]

It is certainly true that the farmers of Alden and Musbury often made a living by combining work on their landholding with some other occupation. Alternatively, if they worked at farming full time, then other members of the household brought in wages by working in another trade. Textiles usually provided another means of earning a living, especially after steam-powered mills sprang up either in the two valleys or in Helmshore. Quarrying also provided an occupation for some farmers and their sons. The 19th century census returns are full of instances where the head of the household was a farmer while his children found work elsewhere. The following examples all come from the 1881 census. John Mawdsley at Hill End (near Higher Tan Pits) and Joseph Haworth at Tor End combined farming with quarrying. At Trees, James Spencer and his wife Mary worked the farm, while their son, John, made his living as a wool sorter. Similarly, at Charity farm in Alden, Thomas Wallwork and his wife were farmers, but had a son who was a stonemason and another son and daughter who were cotton weavers.

QUARRYING AND COALMINING

As we have seen, the people of Musbury and Alden had been accustomed to dig stone on their land and neighbouring commons to use to build their houses, barns and shippons and to enclose their fields. As the pace of industrialisation quickened in the 19th century, the demand for good building stone in Lancashire's towns and villages and beyond changed the character of the local quarrying industry and made a huge impact on the landscape.

In the early 19th century, quarry masters such as the Roscow family of Grane took leases from the Lords of the Manor that gave them rights to get stone in large areas. In 1825, for instance, Richard Roscow agreed to pay £50 a year for all of the quarries in the customary lands, wastes and commons in the manor of Tottington, and in Musbury, Egerton Moss, Boardman Close and Green Haworth Quarry (with certain exceptions). A second lease to Richard and Baxter Roscow in 1835 gave them rights in a similar area for £86 per annum.[32]

The 1848 Ordnance Survey map shows a number of small abandoned quarries in Musbury and Alden, with Musbury Heights quarry being the only one then in use that was of any size. The completion of the Stubbins to Accrington branch of the East Lancashire Railway in 1848 provided a huge impetus to the expansion of the quarrying industry since it became possible to carry away the excellent flag-stone to Manchester, Preston and elsewhere in Lancashire, to Yorkshire, the Midlands and even London. The resulting growth of local quarries was particularly noticeable at Musbury Heights. Here the Roscow family remained in charge until the early 1870s when the firm of Hargreaves and Bolton took over, followed in the early 1900s by the Grane Quarry Co Ltd. Hargreaves and Bolton oversaw the period of greatest expansion. As their workings ate further and further into the tops of the hills, they laid a network of narrow gauge railways to facilitate the movement of stone by locomotive. They also built a stone polishing mill in the middle of the quarry which produced a smooth surface on the flagstones before they were sold. The various branches of the tramway met at the head of a vertical incline above Higher Scars farm in Grane. Here full trucks went down one side of the slope, pulling up empty trucks on the other. From the foot of the incline, a small engine called Roscow (bought in 1877) pulled the loaded trucks to a sliding on the main line at Grane Road. Previously they had been taken by horse and cart to Helmshore station.[33]

In the Alden valley, the quarries were much smaller than Musbury Heights, even at their greatest extent. The largest one was near Alden Mill and belonged to the Rawstron family. It closed in 1872 and was bought by William John Porritt. This purchase gave Porritt access to new reserves of stone, which he used at Sunnybank for the mill and his workers' houses. Alden stone also found its way to the Lancashire coast to the infant resort of St. Anne's. Porritt had taken an interest in the town after he had been invited to attend the laying of the foundation stone of the St Anne's Hotel in 1875.[34] He decided to help to stimulate the growth of the new town by buying a considerable area of land and laying it out in building plots. When not many people came forward to take up these plots, he showed them the way by building houses himself using stone quarried in Alden. He had tramways

FROM HARGREAVES & BOLTON,

Haslingden Grane, Musbury Heights, Edgerton and Pickup Bank Quarries,

HASLINGDEN, *Apl* 19 188 2

WAGON NO.		TON.	C.	Q.
Southport Corp				
15699	44 *yds* 10" x 8" (2) *Cirb*			

Carriage *Paid* To *S'port*

All errors in measurement, &c., not advised on receipt of goods, will not be allowed for at settlement.

Stone from the quarries of Hargreaves and Bolton (including Musbury Heights) went to pave the streets of many Lancashire towns. Here in 1882, kerbs are being sent to Southport.

laid from Alden Quarry and from a smaller one at Black Hile to carry the stone to Sunnybank and thence to the coast.

There has never been any coal mining in Musbury and Alden on a commercial scale, but people worked small outcrops of coal from time to time. The coal that appears in some 17th century inventories such as that of Lawrence Taylor of Musdenhead 1676 may have been dug locally, while later maps and plans pinpoint the location of small coal pits. Thomas Barclay's map of the Honour of Clitheroe dating from about 1810 marks a *'day eye pit'* (a shallow working open to the daylight) in the steep bank above Holcombe Road, opposite the Robin Hood, while another coal pit appears on the six-inch Ordnance Survey map surveyed in 1844 - 47 next to Alden Brook, high above Fall Bank.[35]

NOTES

1   Manor of Accrington records (LRO: DDHCL Liber T, folio 470)
2   Articles of agreement for the lease of Slidings Mill, 1806 (LRO: DDX/118/139/16)
3   Tottington Higher End valuation 1837 (LRO: MBH 5/6)
4   *A map or plan of certain proposed reservoirs to be made on or near the River Irwell* ... (1833) (Rawtenstall Library: RC628.13)
5   James Pigot & Co., *National Commercial directory for Cheshire, Cumberland ... Lancashire* (1828-9); *A map or plan of certain proposed reservoirs to be made on or near the River Irwell* ... (1833) (Rawtenstall Library: RC628.13)
6   C. Aspin, *Haslingden 1800 - 1900*, (1962), p.41
7   1861 census for Musbury (NA: RG 9/3059)
8   Manor of Accrington records (LRO: DDHCL liber NN, folio 214; liber OO, folio 430 and folio 550)
9   *Preston Chronicle* 13th December 1823
10 *Bolton Chronicle* 6th December 1828; 20th December 1828
11 Manor of Accrington records (LRO:DDHCL liber BR, folio 290; liber CY, folio 741); *Bury Times* 2nd August 1879; *Haslingden Guardian* 16th December 1893

[12] A. Muir, *The history of Porritts and Spencer Limited,* (1966, unpublished), pp. 70 - 71; Manor of Accrington records (LRO: DDHCL liber EI, folios 265 and 724; liber BV, folio 255)

[13] *Bury Times* 1st June 1867

[14] Midge Hole or Wood Bank Mill was bought in 1878. See Manor of Accrington records (LRO: DDHCL liber CT, folio 1231)

[15] Dr. G. H. Tupling's interview with Jack Lord, 31st March 1921 (Helmshore Local History Society collection); *Bury Times* 8th May 1875; *Bacup Times* 5th June 1875

[16] *Haslingden and Rawtenstall Express* 4th August 1866

[17] Manor of Accrington records (LRO: DDHCL liber DL, folio 343)

[18] *Rossendale Free Press* 6th November 1886; Haslingden Local Board Highways and Building Committee 3rd May 1888 (LRO: MBH 3/6)

[19] Dissolved companies files (NA: BT31/3867/24392); *Cotton Factory Times* 17th May 1889

[20] *Bacup Times* 20th July 1889; *Haslingden Guardian* 24th July 1896

[21] Manor of Accrington records (LRO: DDHCL liber BM, folio 395; liber BW, folio 280; liber CK, folio 1308); *The Times* 6th August 1862; C. Aspin, *op. cit.,* p. 51; *Cotton Factory Times* 5th May 1893

[22] *Bury Times* 12th July 1873

[23] *Bury Times* 22nd June 1878

[24] Courtesy of C. Aspin

[25] *Bury Times* 19th November 1881

[26] Manor of Accrington records (LRO: DDHCL liber PP, folio 61; liber QQ, folio 143; liber WW, folio 71). The 1841 census returns for Musbury record that two cottages were being built at Carr Lane.

[27] *Bacup Times* 4th October 1890, 18th October 1890; *Accrington Times* 4th October 1890

[28] Dr. G. H. Tupling's interview with John Mort 19th December 1920 (Helmshore Local History Society collection)

[29] P. Stephens and R. Hawkin, *Historical Notices of Helmshore and Musbury,* Part VI (1929), pp. 89 - 90

[30] Musbury Tithe File 1844 (NA: IR 18/4178/8155)

[31] G. Beesley, *A report of the state of agriculture in Lancashire,* (1849), pp. 6 - 7

[32] Lease of coal mines, quarries etc. (LRO: DDHCL uncat. box 133)

[33] *Bury Times* 21st July 1877

[34] A. Muir, *op. cit.,* chapter XXIX

ALL CHANGE

B Y THE EARLY 1900s, the focus of housing and industry had switched away from the outlying parts of Musbury and Alden to the village of Helmshore, which had started to grow in the early 19th century. The change had begun following the construction of the turnpike road (now Holcombe Road) under an 1810 Act of Parliament. The road cut through the edge of the old deer park and before long saw rows of cottages built along its length. This was especially the case where the road left behind a small piece of land at the side of a field. The Turners used just such a piece of land as the site for their cottages at Tan Pits in the 1820s and there are others at Hollin Bank and Weir Foot. Later in the 19th century, rows of terraced houses, many of them built by Helmshore Co-op, joined these cottages. Other buildings too appeared at the side of the road, including the village school built in 1815 on a site now part of the wooded area at the entrance to Wood Bank and the Primitive and Wesleyan Methodist chapels.

The railway (opened in 1848) also exerted a strong pull away from the two valleys and, although the new Anglican parish formed in 1844 took its name from Musbury, the site chosen for its church a few years later was outside the township. The year 1883 marked the demise of Musbury as a unit of local government when it came under the jurisdiction of Haslingden Local Board and thereafter it was counted as simply part of Helmshore.

INDUSTRY'S DECLINE

The early years of the 20th century were, in general, ones of prosperity and expansion for the four remaining Musbury mills. At Sunnybank, additions included a new felting room in 1907 and a carding room in 1913 and at the same time, Oliver Porritt began to reorganise the mill, moving the weaving department to the top floor, which could accommodate some of the widest looms in the world. In 1914 Sunnybank became the headquarters of Porritts and Spencer Ltd, a new company combining the forces of the businesses set up by different branches of the Porritt family and their former manager, J. H. Spencer. Oliver Porritt continued to buy new machines after the First World War and by the end of the 1930s, these had required a new felt room, additions to the finishing department and a new inspection and stock room.

The other Sunnybank Mill at Tan Pits continued to work on a more modest scale, with James Barlow's grandchildren making the business into a private limited company in 1909. On occasion, the firm's Albert Mill found itself pressed into

Sunnybank from the air in 1968. Within a few years, nothing remained of the mill, which had provided work for hundreds of Helmshore people.

service as the venue for special events. James Albert Barlow and his bride, Florence Taylor, held their wedding reception there in 1904, and two years later a bazaar in the mill raised money to pay for the extension to Helmshore Liberal Club. The company made the only substantial addition to the main mill in 1950 when they built a winding room between the spinning room and the weaving shed. This allowed cops from the mules to be carried by conveyor belt into the new building where they were wound on to cones and then carried to the weavers. These 'pirned' cops had the advantage of being twice the size of the originals and therefore lasting longer. The mill continued to use cotton waste to make sheetings and similar products and it was often said in the village that if a newly-married couple received a pair of Barlow's sheets and a pair of Porritts' blankets then they were set up for life.[1]

Benjamin Haworth sold Park Mill to J.H. Birtwistle and Company Ltd in 1906 and in 1914, the new owners built another extension overlooking Park Street. The company used Park Mill for both spinning and weaving until 1956 when they centralised weaving at Grane Road Mill. New machines installed at Park Mill in 1964 produced acrylic coloured yarns for knitting and weaving and at the same time the mill became the first in the country to switch to working 142 hours a week on a four shift system.[2]

Middle Mill's fortunes continued to be somewhat mixed in the first half of the 20th century. The Middle Mill Manufacturing Company wound up in 1896, and the Helmshore Manufacturing Company took its place. Like its predecessor, the new firm was set up by a group of working men, most of whom were employed in the cotton trade. The company left the village in 1911 but continued to run mills in Ramsbottom until the early 1930s. Its successor at Middle Mill, the Torside Manufacturing Company, had family connections with the mill going back into the 19th century. Its directors included John Arthur Witham and his brother-in-law, Ralph V. S. Houghton. John's father, Joseph Clarke Witham, had married the daughter of John and Betty Ashworth and had worked as manager at Middle Mill until 1877. The Withams inherited the mill after Betty Ashworth's death and continued to have an interest in it until the Second World War. It closed in 1924 and for a time was taken over by J. H. Birtwistle Ltd. The depressed state of the cotton trade forced its closure again by May 1931, throwing about 180 people out of work. Not long afterwards, several workpeople approached Jack Witham (John Arthur's son) to see if he could restart the mill. At a meeting in October 1931, more than 130 former employees agreed that they would work for twelve months with four shillings in the pound deducted from their wages to help to get the mill going again. At the end of the year, they would get back their money or be given shares in a new limited company that would be set up to run the mill. The generally depressed state

An unusual view of the mills at Tan Pits in 1905. Just beyond the roof of Spring Hill Wesleyan chapel is Betty Ashworth's weaving shed, with the older part of Middle Mill behind. On the left is Barlow's Sunnybank Mill, with Park Mill's chimney prominent in the centre of the picture.

of the cotton trade at the time and an industry-wide strike in 1932 meant that the new firm (also called the Torside Manufacturing Company) did not get going until 1933.[3]

By May 1936, the mill was up for sale again but there were no takers and the machinery was sold off piecemeal. Shortly before the outbreak of the Second World War, the Cotton Storage Co Ltd was using the buildings to store materials, but in 1941, Haslingden Borough Council bought the mill and rented it to the London firm of Industrial and Mechanical Engineers Ltd. This company stayed throughout the war years making munitions and by the summer of 1941, Middle Mill had become Wavell Works, no doubt in honour of General Wavell whose military successes in North Africa were in the news at the time.[4]

After the war, the mill became the home of the research centre for a group of textile machinery manufacturing companies, including Platt Brothers, Howard and Bullough and Dobson and Barlow. TMM (Research) Ltd controlled the Helmshore mill and for more than thirty years, the company carried out experiments into the production of yarn and the development of new machines. In 1956, they expanded into a new building on the opposite side of Holcombe Road, which housed the Technological, Technical Economy, and Technical Information and Patents departments. Two hundred and fifty people worked for TMM in its heyday but by the early 1980s, the decline of the textile industry had taken its toll. Wavell Works closed in 1981 and the 1950s extension in the following year.[5]

The old buildings became industrial units, housing a number of different businesses, the largest of which was the travel firm Airtours, which eventually took over nearly the entire mill. The company demolished Betty Ashworth's weaving shed in 1990, replacing it with a new reception building and several new blocks at the rear. Hamilton McBride, a firm of household bedding manufacturers, moved into the 1956 building in 1983 and stayed for nearly ten years.

The 1970s and 1980s also saw the end of the other mills that stood within the boundaries of the old Musbury township. Sunnybank Mill was the first to go. Porritts and Spencer had merged with the Scapa Group in 1970 and the mill no longer had a place in the new concern's plans. It was put up for sale but no buyers came forward and various schemes for its use came to nothing. Eventually the demolition men moved in and on a rainy Sunday afternoon in July 1977, a crowd of villagers gathered at Wood Bank to watch the felling of the 188ft high chimney, almost the last remnant of the huge complex.

James Barlow's Sunnybank and Albert Mills closed in 1981, a couple of years after Taylor and Hartley of Westhoughton had taken over the firm. The 1820s dye-works buildings with their various extensions, including the 1893 weaving shed, were demolished, but Albert Mill found a new use as a pine furniture shop. Just down the road, Park Mill worked on for a couple of more years. J.H. Birtwistle Ltd announced twenty redundancies in October 1980, but hoped that the transfer of knitting machinery to Park Mill from a mill at Freckleton would help matters.

Staff hard at work in one of TMM's laboratories in the 1950s.

However, when Holme Spring Mill became vacant next to the company's Grane Road Mill, they took the decision to concentrate production on one site and closed Park Mill in 1984. Like Middle Mill, it found a new use as units.[6]

FARMING

For much of the 20th century, Musbury and Alden farmers continued to make a living largely by selling milk, butter and eggs to the households of Helmshore and Haslingden. They soon found, however, that their activities were subject to more and more rules and regulations. Haslingden Borough Council's sanitary inspectors acquired powers to visit farms, inspect shippons and order changes to those that fell short of the new standards. The milk offered for sale also came under scrutiny as Lawrence Barnes of Kiln Field found to his cost in June 1906. His son, Rowland, was delivering milk in Haslingden when he was stopped and a sample of milk taken for analysis. The County Analyst found that it was deficient in cream and concluded that it must have been skimmed before being sold. Rowland countered that he and his sister Alice had milked their twelve cows at six in the morning and poured the milk straight into the kit on the milk float. The magistrates would have none of this and fined Lawrence, although they took into consideration the fact that he had been farming for thirty-three years and had no previous convictions and imposed a penalty of just £2 and costs.[7]

John Berry from Higher Tan Pits delivering milk at Whitecroft in January 1940.

New legislation also required farmers to register with the borough council as cow keepers, dairymen or purveyors of milk and the farms in Alden and Musbury soon appear in the lists. For example, in 1915 William Collins of Park House, Joseph Whipp of Tor End and William and Rowland Barnes of Higher Park House all signed up to the scheme. A new grading system introduced in the early 1920s also allowed farmers to apply for licences to sell milk described as either Certified Milk, Graded A (Tuberculin Tested) Milk or Grade A Milk. The establishment of the Milk Marketing Board in 1933 meant that local farmers could sell their surplus milk to the Board instead of using it for butter making or calf rearing. This arrangement provided them with a regular income to supplement their sale of milk in Helmshore and Haslingden. From 1936, the Milk Marketing Board redesignated Grade A milk as 'Accredited' and paid a bonus to any farmers selling such milk.

One man who certainly believed in the quality of his milk and other products was John Berry who farmed at Higher Tan Pits in the 1920s and '30s. He set out their merits in an advertisement, which he placed in local newspapers in 1934. It begins:

My two Specialities are two Perfect Foods that Chemists haven't conquered. The Cow beats the Laboratory, so does the Hen. Clean Bottled Milk and New Laid Hen and Duck Eggs.

The advertisement goes on to give the advice that:

If you are corpulent, well, cut one meal a day out and take in its place One Bottle of my Milk and One Egg split in same (a Country Egg, with a bright yellow yolk, not a pale-yoked egg from a pen). You will suddenly become active, and consequently you will want to knock about more and you will naturally become normal without any hard labour.[8]

THE PORRITT ESTATE

By the time William John Porritt died in 1896, he had been able to buy many of the farms in Musbury and Alden, making him the largest landowner in the area. His estate passed jointly to his sons, William John the younger and Harold, and then to his grandson Oliver William, all of whom took a keen interest in its day-to-day running. Both William John the elder and Harold were enthusiastic tree planters whose schemes completely transformed Sunnybank into the heavily wooded area we know today. In the 1880s, William John had also turned his attention to the shelf of land at the back of Tor. One visitor said:

> These tops are being rapidly brought under cultivation. Flame and smoke were ascending from their coarse grasses, while in other parts furrows of newly-ploughed land were lying open to the pulverising effects of the atmosphere. The smell of the peaty soil was fragrant as spices wafted from some southern shore, and the burning wicks gave a pungency delightful to the senses.[9]

Eventually there were three shippons, a calf house, a three-stalled stable and a Dutch barn at The Exe, as this part of the estate became known.[10]

Harold continued his father's work and on his death in 1910, the Rev. John Phillipson, minister of Helmshore Primitive Methodist chapel, said:

> He loved to hear the clink of the mason's hammer and chisel as the stones were shaped for their place in some building; and in his own mind he was constructing and planning to make "the waste places into cities of habitation." During the last few years in Helmshore, old houses have been pulled down and new ones built, crooked roads have been made straight, and rough places have been made smooth, trees planted, until our village has become one of the beauty spots of the district.[11]

Harold was responsible for the demolition of some of the old farms on the estate, such as Black Hill and shortly before his death, he began to extend and modernise the family home at Tor Side House. His son, Oliver William, completed the work in the following year.

The farms in Alden flourished in the 1920s under the care of Oliver and his second wife Katherine (Kitty). She was the daughter of William John Porritt the younger and had become interested in dairy farming and poultry rearing while growing up at Red Hall, Ballycarry in Northern Ireland. Great House became the stock farm where they raised pedigree Shorthorns, including a prize-winning bull called Musbury Magnet. By 1923, there were over 200 head of cattle on the estate, some of which provided milk for the dairy farm at Alden. Milk produced here was sold in Haslingden and the surrounding area, while cream went for sale in several

Oliver William and Katherine Porritt at the door of Tor Side House in about 1921.

nearby towns and to St Anne's, where housewives could buy it within three hours of milking time at Alden. The Porritts also came to an arrangement with Haslingden Corporation to supply 'certified milk' to nursing and expectant mothers within the borough.[12]

Trees farm, on the road up to Tor End, became the estate's poultry farm where some forty breeding pens and six 'intensive' houses were the home to hundreds of Wyandottes and Rhode Island Reds. Porritt employed a Miss Hutchinson from the County Council's farm at Hutton to manage the farm and put into operation up-to-date ideas on the breeding and rearing of poultry. From Trees, adult hens also went to stock other farms on the estate.

The Porritts also had rights to shoot game on the surrounding moorland and employed John Mort as a gamekeeper. Causeway End, right at the top of Musbury, became their shooting box, with the butts towards Hoglowe Pike. They built kennels for their dogs in the garden of Longfield House and it was here that Oliver and Kitty bred prize-winning dogs for a number of years. A visitor in 1904 said:

> The kennels stand on a gentle slope at the bottom of Longfield, and comprise a substantially built erection which possesses every up-to-date convenience. The purest of spring-water is carried in pipes through the kennel-yards, and the practically inexhaustible supply of water is one of the greatest recommendations of the locality of the kennels. In other respects, however, they are well-favoured, for they are situate in an area which is admirably suited to the requirements of the animals, and, accompanied by their keeper, they can roam for miles over the breezy moorland estate … Even in the commodious kennels, however, the dogs have a comparative absence of restraint, for each kennel has a spacious yard, from which during the daytime the animals have every opportunity for observation of their splendid surroundings. They were quick to note the approach of visitors, and for some time prior to our arrival at the kennels the air resounded with the exuberant welcome they extended, and the noise was distinctly reminiscent of a dog-show. The kennels were found to be wonderfully clean, the concrete floors being tidily swept, while everything appeared to be as comfortable as the art of man could make it. The running water dripped with cheery persistence into the various receptacles, while the food-troughs bore evidence of recent replenishment, and the dogs were consequently in satisfied and philosophical mood. The sleeping apartments are accommodating enough for the most fastidious and exacting animal, and contain raised sleeping berths with an abundance of straw.[13]

When the visit was made, all of the dogs were Irish setters, including the bitch 'Molly Machree' which had won many prizes including two firsts at the Ladies' Kennel Association Show at Regent's Park before Queen Alexandra. A few years later, the Porritts switched to breeding and showing Irish terriers, again with a great deal of success. One dog 'Barlae Brickbat' won twenty-two championships and more than 2,000 prizes.[14]

Oliver and Kitty were the last of the Porritts to live in Helmshore. They left Tor Side in 1929 for their estate near Stranraer. The contents of the house were auctioned off and the building itself rented to the Hon. John Kemp, son of Lord

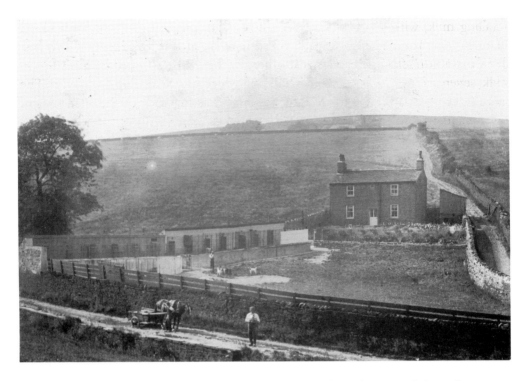

Longfield House and the Porritts' kennels in Musbury in the early years of the 20th century.

Rochdale. In the summer of 1944, Oliver and Kitty returned to Helmshore and lived at 'Moorfields', just below Tor Side, but they left the village again in 1946 and moved to Oswestry where Oliver died in 1948. Tor Side House became a country club and in April 1950, hosted the BBC programme '*Thé Dansant*'.

HANDS TO THE PLOUGH

At the beginning of the Second World War, the Government set up County War Agricultural Executive Committees whose job it was to try to increase food production. One of the ways they sought to do this was by overseeing a ploughing-up campaign which saw fields and meadows turned from grassland to arable. Later in the war, the Committees also carried out a National Farm Survey to provide information for post-war agricultural planning. The resulting records, which survive in the National Archives, provide us with a snapshot of the farms in Musbury and Alden in the early 1940s.

As we shall see, by 1939 the farms in the upper end of Musbury had fallen out of use and so were not included in the survey. The remaining working farms in the valley were Kiln Field, Higher and Middle Park House, Middle Hollin Bank and Carr Lane. In Alden, there were Great House, Alden and Cronkshaw Fold, with Trees and Tor End completing the list. Most of the farmers said they made a living retailing milk, with dairy cows and poultry making up the bulk of their stock. Naturally, the largest herds of cattle were at Great House and Alden, but Ernest Taylor at Kiln Field also had a sizeable herd with twenty-four cows and heifers in milk, seven cows in calf, a bull and a bull calf, which he was rearing for service. The large flock of hens at Great House (150 birds) was matched by Fred Barlow's at Middle Hollin Bank where he also had five ducks. Ernest Townley at Cronkshaw Fold had ninety hens, and even John Mort at Carr Lane, who also worked as a wool sorter, had sixty hens and five geese.

Great House had a flock of sheep (244 in all), as did John Seed's farm at Tor End (183). The only man to keep pigs was Ernest Taylor who had a barren sow for fattening and eleven other pigs at Kiln Field. Apart from Starkie Downham at Trees, everyone had one or more horses for farm work, although John Mort made do with a donkey. Some of the returns record the beginning of changes that were to alter farming completely after the war. For example, Starkie Downham had two tractors (but no horses), while Ernest Townley used a converted car for some field work as well as his two mares. By February 1943, Great House had converted from milking cows by hand to using electricity.

Ernest Taylor and Roy Gibbons muckspreading on land at Kiln Field, which they had ploughed up to help the war effort in 1944.

The National Farm Survey records also reveal how the ploughing-up campaign affected the farms in Musbury and Alden. A return made on 4th June 1941 gives details of the arable crops farmers were growing alongside their hay meadows and permanent pasture. Several had sown oats in varying quantities ranging from three-quarters of an acre at Cronkshaw Fold to ten acres at Great House and nearly all of the farms had some land given over to kale. Turnip and swedes for fodder made an appearance at Trees, Kiln Field, Park House, Cronkshaw Fold and Carr Lane, while there were 2 acres of vetches at Rake Foot, 2½ acres of peas and oats for silage at Park House and a quarter of an acre of mangolds at Cronkshaw Fold. Some farmers also reported that they were growing their own potatoes, usually a half or a quarter of an acre, although Starkie Downham had put in half an acre of first earlies and 1¼ acres of main crop and second earlies at Trees.

THE EXPERIMENTAL FARM

Oliver Porritt sold most of his property in Alden to Porritts and Spencer Ltd in 1932 and they in turn sold it to the Ministry of Agriculture in 1951. The Government had been looking for a large area of land somewhere in the Pennines to use as an Experimental Husbandry Farm and the 350 acres or so of Porritt property in Alden proved an ideal acquisition. Great House EHF opened in 1952,

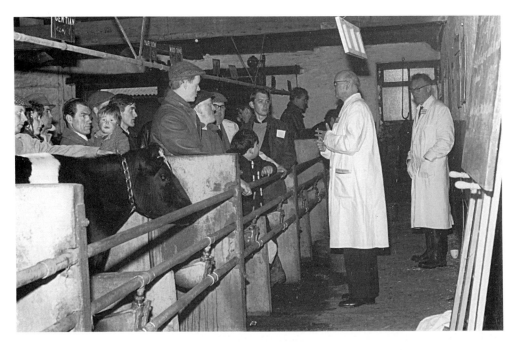

An open day at Great House Experimental Husbandry Farm in the 1960s. On the right is Harry Mudd, farm director for twenty-eight years.

with Tor Side House as offices and living accommodation. Under the directorship of Harry Mudd, work at Great House started with adapting the old farm buildings and draining and fencing the land before concentrating on experiments dealing with the feeding and management of dairy cows, sheep and pigs. The farm also monitored environmental pollution, recording the soot and sulphur dioxide content of the air and their effect on grass growth. Beginning with a staff of just two, Great House eventually employed more than thirty people and for nearly thirty years offered help and advice to Pennine hill farmers.[15]

The farm fell victim to Government cuts in 1981 and closed in the following year. In June 1982, Edenfield farmer George Holt and property developer John Ashworth bought the property at auction. Great House continued as a working farm while the old barns at Halliwells, Trickling Water and Fall Bank became homes. George Holt's brother-in-law, Neil Edmondson, bought Alden Farm and here too the house and barn (converted into houses) were sold off separately. The third piece of the estate, Tor Side House, also passed into private ownership.[16]

GATHERING WATER

Several dry years in the 1920s prompted Bury and District Joint Water Board to approach Oliver Porritt with a view to using Musbury to collect water. Between 1921 and 1927, he allowed the Board to take water from the lodge at Hare Clough through a pipe down the valley where it met one of the water mains from Grane. In 1934, he agreed to sell his land in the valley - some 806 acres - for £8,000. This acquisition allowed the Board to lay a new eighteen-inch diameter pipe from Hare Clough to carry the water around Hill End and into the Ogden Reservoir.[17]

A more ambitious plan came forward when the Irwell Valley Water Board (the Bury Board's successor) decided to look into the possibility of building a reservoir in Musbury. They estimated that such an undertaking could hold 222,000,000 gallons of water and in the autumn of 1954, they began test drilling to see if the underlying rock formation made the valley suitable for flooding. By 1959, the estimated cost of the project had risen to £1M and, partly because of the water shortage caused by the hot, dry summer of that year, the Board negotiated to become partners and shareholders in Manchester Corporation's Haweswater pipeline. They could take one million gallons of water a day from the pipeline and so abandoned plans for flooding Musbury.[18]

Although the Musbury reservoir was never built, the fact that much of the valley had become a water-gathering ground meant that the working lives of most of the small farms had ended. The abandoned houses, farm buildings and field walls fell into ruin and the land reverted to rough pasture used only for sheep grazing. Much of Musbury and Alden became places for the people of Helmshore to enjoy a walk or a picnic. The Earl of Lincoln's deer park, once the pleasure ground for a select few, could now be enjoyed by all.

Test drilling for the proposed Musbury reservoir taking place on the side of Tor, opposite
Longfield House, in the autumn of 1954.

NOTES

1   *Haslingden Guardian* 10th June 1904; 20th April 1906; *Haslingden Observer* 22nd April 1950

2   Manor of Accrington records (LRO: DDHCL Liber FB, folio 547); *Ramsbottom Observer* 26th June 1914; *Burnley Evening Star* 9th February 1970

3   Dissolved companies files (NA: BT 31/15618/48019; BT 31/19933/114849; BT 31/33481/283168); *Haslingden Gazette* 4th October 1924; *Haslingden Observer* 17th July 1926, 21st July 1934

4   *Ramsbottom Observer* 1st May 1936; Haslingden Borough Council minutes: General Purposes Committee 13th December 1939, 22nd January 1941; Industrial Development Committee 17th June 1941

5   *T.M.M. (Research) Limited October 1958*; *Rossendale Free Press* 20th December 1908, 1st July 1981, 8th August 1981

6   *Haslingden Borough News* 5th May 1981; *Haslingden Observer* 1st October 1980; *Haslingden Borough News* 26th July 1983

7   *Haslingden Guardian* 3rd August 1906

8   The advertisement seems to have appeared in the *Haslingden Borough News*

9   Marshall Mather, J., *Rambles Round Rossendale* (1888), p.105

10 Survey of the Helmshore Estate belonging to O. W. Porritt 1922 (Helmshore Local History Society)

11 *Haslingden Guardian* 5th August 1910

12 *Haslingden Gazette* 10th February 1923; Haslingden Borough Council, Health and Sanitary Committee minutes, 20th November 1929

13 *Ramsbottom Observer* 8th July 1904

14 *Ramsbottom Observer* 14th June 1912

15 *Haslingden Borough News* 3rd June 1980

16 *Haslingden Borough News* 3rd November 1981; 1st June 1982

17 *Haslingden Observer* 11th August 1934

18 *Haslingden Observer* 25th September 1954; 12th September 1959

A MUSBURY MISCELLANY

THE MUSBURY 'BATTLE AXE'

IN 1982, Mr. Jim Ingham of Park Crescent, Haslingden was out walking his dog near Higher Tan Pits when he stumbled across a stone implement, which proved to be a Bronze Age axe-hammer. Fashioned in coarse granite, the implement weighs 5lb 4oz and is 8in long. It was probably made in the Lake District or North Wales and would have been used for breaking up the ground.

HORSE THIEVES IN 1635

On Monday 2nd March 1635, James Rothwell of Musbury went out to look for his horse, *'a greay Nagg',* and found it missing. A couple of days later, he heard that Thomas Hamer of Buckden had been seen riding through Haslingden on a horse which sounded very much like the one that was missing. Furthermore, Hamer and

The Bronze Age implement discovered by chance in Musbury in 1982.

his brothers John and Roger had travelled to Whalley where they spent forty shillings. Rothwell decided to voice his suspicions to a local Justice of the Peace who called a number of other people to give evidence. The first witness was Michael Haworth of Haslingden who had told James Rothwell that he had seen Thomas Hamer riding the horse and that he (Hamer) had tried to disguise himself by means of *'a Cloth tyed on his face and his hatt puld downe.'* Haworth also said that he himself had been going to Ribchester on foot *'yᵗ day after that the last great frost begun to breake'*. The Hamers had overtaken him on the outskirts of Haslingden a little after sunrise. They were all on horseback and had a fourth horse with them. He said that either John or Roger Hamer was on a grey nag.

Another witness, Christopher Nuttall of New Hall Hey, said that he too had seen the brothers riding through Haslingden leading another horse behind them. He knew Roger Hamer and had spoken to him, but Hamer had a white cloth tied across his face and did not reply. The next day, Nuttall saw the Hamers again in Whalley and asked Roger why he had ignored him the day before. Hamer's reply was that Nuttall's *'Complexcion was much altered … and therefore hee knew him not.'*

The Hamers' version of events was that they had travelled to Whalley to collect some wheat, which Thomas had bought. John said that they took four horses, all of which belonged to their father. When they arrived at Whalley, they dined at John Watt's house. Once they had concluded their business, they loaded the wheat on to three of the horses and John and Thomas set out with them, taking turns to ride on the fourth horse. Roger stayed behind in Whalley. John said one of the horses had since been sold, but that of the remaining three, two were bay and the other was *'a kinde of a blacke somewhat gryseld.'* Thomas Hamer corroborated this and added that they had only spent 12d at Whalley, 3d each for their dinners and the remainder in drink.[1]

John Hamer was summonsed to appear at the Easter Quarter Sessions in Salford, but the case has left no further trace in the court records and it may be that the Justices decided that the evidence was too conflicting to proceed.

THE MUSBURY BURYIN'

Major David Halstead, the Haslingden historian, recounts the following story in his 'Yarns and Recollections', which were published in the local newspaper in the 1920s. He does not give a date for when the event took place, but said that it happened during the incumbency of the Rev. William Gray who was at Haslingden between 1813 and 1847:

There had been an exceedingly hard and long winter, with heavy snow which had drifted in many places to several feet. A farmer had died at one of the most inaccessible farms on Musbury Heights. The curate had been warned several times of the intention of the family to bury their father, but it was found impossible to traverse the rough countryside, and the funeral cortege had to turn back more than once.

At last one of the sons succeeded in getting through the snow to warn Mr. Gray that they had finally decided to force their way to the churchyard (at Haslingden) on the following day.

"Yo' see, Mr. Gray," he said, "we've laithed all the relatives five times already, an' as th' moon war at th' full last week, we killed three fat pigs, as we couldn't howd 'em off any longer as th' provin wur o' done. Th' owd chap's bin in un eowt ov th' bacon kist for o'er six weeks, un aw'm tryin' to feight my way back wi' another cob o' sawt."

The above story was told to me as having actually happened, the body having to be "salted" owing to the impossibility of traversing the four miles of rough country roads.[2]

THE WOMAN OF MUSBURY

In the two years that followed the ending of the Napoleonic Wars, Lancashire textile workers faced increasing hardships as the Corn Laws kept up the price of food, thousands of demobilised soldiers and sailors flooded the labour market and the Government cancelled contracts for cloth. To make matters worse, employers lowered wages claiming it was the only way they could withstand increasing competition. By March 1817, the situation had become so bad that the workers decided to stage a march to London to present petitions to the Prince Regent. This plan alarmed the authorities who moved quickly to stop the march. They also suspended the Habeas Corpus Act, a move that drove many of the reformers into hiding. Their number included Samuel Bamford, a weaver from Middleton. He and his friend Joseph Healey made their way secretly to Holcombe by way of Ashworth Moor and Edenfield. Here they entered a public house and took some refreshment. He recounts what happened next:

We were talking on various matters, when the door was opened, and a personally fine looking woman with an infant at the breast, advanced timidly, and said she wished to speak to the overseer. Her outer garments were of very homely material, being seemingly cotton fents dyed blue, but neatly fitting her person, and very clean. She had a pair of light clogs on her feet, and her stockings were, I could perceive, well darned above the buckles. Her petticoat and bed gown, were of the same blue cotton, and the latter was open at the bosom, where a fine boy lay smiling at his pap. Her apron was striped calico; and her head gear consisted of a striped napkin, apparently also a fent, over a mob cap, very white; from beneath which a lock of black hair had escaped, and hung as if in contrast with a bosom of as pure white as ever appertained to human nature. Her features were also handsome; her cheeks were faintly tinged on a very pale ground. Her mouth was somewhat wan; she seemed rather exhausted; and as she stood, the tears came into her dark and modest eyes.

"Weer dusto com fro," asked the overseer; "an' wot dusto want? Theawrt a new un at ony rate," he continued. She said she came from Musbury, and wanted relief for her husband, herself and two children, besides the infant. "An' wot dun yo doo for a livin?" interrogated the overseer. They wove calico, she said, when they could get work and were able; but the children at home were ill of the measles; the shopkeeper had refused them any more credit, and her husband had "wurched for 'em till he fell off his looms, and wur beginning' o' th' feyver th' docthur said so." "Hang those docthurs," said the overseer, "why conno they let foke dee when thur time comes." "I hope he'll no' dee yet" said the poor woman, tears streaming in plenty. "I think he'd com reawnd iv yod nobbut let us have a trifle o' summat to carry on wi'; an' iv yo win (intreatingly) I'll hie me whom, an' I'll put th' chylt i' th' keyther an' set at yon wark, an' I'll finish it myself; an' we'n not trouble yo ogen unless we'en sum new misfortin'."

The overseer asked the farmers, who it appeared were rate-payers, what they thought of the case; and the result was that he gave two shillings, and promised to call and see the family. But she must tell her husband he must not begin of the fever. "Its o' idlety, idlety; an' iv th' paupers o' th' teawn yerd at he geet owt wi' bein ill o' th' feyver, they'd o' begin." "Nowe, nowe, theyd'n ha no fevers i' their teawnship." She took the money, curtseyed, and thanked the overseer and rate-payers. One of them said she had been "a decent wench"; he knew her father in better days, and offered her a glass of the warm ale, which she put to her lips, and swallowed a small quantity. Her cheeks turned deathly pale; she put out her hand as if her sight was gone; her grasp relaxed; the child dropped on Healey's knee, and I caught the fainting woman in my arms. "Hoos clem'd to dyeth," said one of the rate-payers. "Hoos as dyed as a dur nail," said the other. "I didno' deny her relief," said the overseer. The doctor handed the child to the landlady, and called for some brandy, which was brought, together with a sharp smelling bottle which was applied, but there was not any perceptible breathing; and she shrunk down seated upon the floor, I kneeling and still keeping her in a leaning posture.

Healey chafed her temples with the liquor, sprinkled her face with water, opened her hands, and tried to get a drop of liquid into her mouth, but her teeth were set. "Poor thing," said the doctor, "she must have been very ill." "Hoos dun for i' this ward," said one of the men. "I relieft hur," said the overseer, "for I seed hoo'r none eawr reggilur paupers." "We shan ha' to have an inquest," said the constable. "Moor expence, an' moor," said the overseer; "but they conno say 'at I neglected 'em, con they." Whilst these observations and many others were passing, the features of the sufferer became less rigid; the jaw relaxed; a drop of brandy and water was administered; a slight tinge of pink appeared on her cheeks; the chafings and smellings were continued; a sigh after some time escaped, and in a minute or two those dark fringed eyed unclosed; she looked inquiringly around, and soon appeared to comprehend her situation. In a short time she was restored; her child was again pressed to her bosom; the two shillings were made up to five; she took a cup of warm tea with the family; and in another hour she was slowly wending up the hill towards Musbury.[3]

THE ROAD THAT NEVER WAS

In 1824, a group of local manufactures and landowners got together to promote a new turnpike road which would shorten the journey from Haslingden to Bolton. They proposed a route through Musbury that seems quite extraordinary, considering the gradients involved and the difficult terrain it would have had to cross. From Three Lane Ends, opposite the Holden Arms, the road cut across the meadows down to the River Ogden, crossing at a point now beneath the Holden Wood Reservoir. It then climbed up to Hill End, following the hillside around to Higher Tan Pits and Rushy Leach. Here it made a sharp left turn and followed the line of the old park ditch before climbing to Causeway End. The road then struck

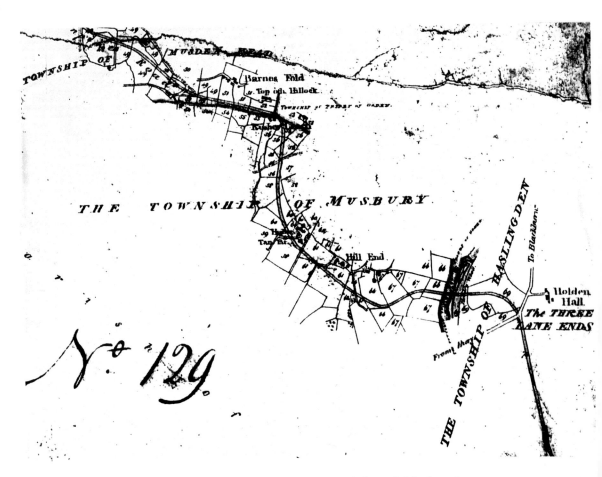

The proposed route of the turnpike road through Musbury in 1824.
[*Source: Lancashire Record Office PDS/31*]

out across the open moor at Musdenhead, went down the hillside at the other side and joined the existing road just to the north of Edgworth. The trustees went to the trouble and expense of having the route properly surveyed and a map prepared and in 1825, obtained an Act of Parliament to allow the scheme to go ahead. However, nothing further came of the venture.[4]

LOST IN THE SNOW

In his book *Holcombe Long Ago* published in 1902, the Rev. Henry Dowsett, recounts the story of Richmael Smith who lived at Middle Doe in Alden in the early 19th century. She died in tragic circumstances in March 1838. (Dowsett mistakenly gives the year as 1837). According to the story passed down to Dowsett, she set out one evening to borrow candles from a neighbour '*but the gloaming deepened into blackest night, and, losing her way on her return, she wandered in the fast-falling snow over Alden Ratchers towards Edgworth, till at length, sinking from exhaustion, she died upon the Moor.*' It took three days for her family and friends to find her body and eventually it was discovered '*through the sagacity of a dog.*'

At the inquest held at Knowsley Barn, Edgworth (another name for the Dog and Grouse public house, now called the Toby Inn), the coroner recorded that she had been found dead in a field at Edgworth on 5th March and had apparently starved to death. She was just 24 years old. The witnesses were Peter Smith, her father, who no doubt came to identify the body, and a man called Thomas Entwistle, who may have been the person who found her. No report of the circumstances of her death or of the inquest found their way into local newspapers, so we can only assume that the details Dowsett records were passed on to him by word of mouth. Richmael Smith was buried at St. Anne's, Tottington on 10th March 1838.[5]

WIFE SELLING AT THE WHITE HORSE

The following report appeared in the *Bury Times* 13th November 1869:

A circumstance transpired in the immediate neighbourhood of Musbury the other Saturday evening, which is certainly of too remarkable a character to pass by unnoticed and find a mere resting place in the agglomeration of unchronicled episodes. Two of the neighbouring farmers – our sympathy for their future welfare only induces us to withhold their names – were soaking the inner mortal with considerably more than a "drop o' th' craythur" at a well-known hostelry in the district, which, in addition to the "nut-brown ale" within doors, aspires still further to a connection with the animal race by means of its signboard, which has "weather'd many a storm," and the stimulated couple had become "fou and unco' happy," one of them, who is a trifle over thirty years of age, and about two years the senior of his pot companion, made a *bona fide* promise to sell him his wife, "bairns" (of whom there are two or three), the farm, and the entire stock for something like £300. The offer was accepted by the junior agriculturalist, who, still in the domains of bachelordom, probably thought this was an admirable opportunity of increasing his possession, animate and inanimate. The sum of ten shillings was laid down as a deposit, and eventually the couple separated. By some means or other the wife who had been so unceremoniously sold and bought without her opinion being consulted got wind of the transaction, much to the alarm of her liege lord, who received sundry dis-edifying admonitions for his fickle affection, and was assured by his stout-hearted "better-half" that if "So-and-so" had really bought her he would have to make that his habitation, for she was determined not to "flit." The poor fellow, now that "reason had resumed her throne" was the most penitent of sinners; and the following day had not far advanced before he had an interview with his younger "brother chip" who also seemed to have deeply repented of the bargain he had made, and appeared more desirous of "driving his cattle to another market." By mutual consent the agreement was cancelled, and the virtue of a gallon of ale was speedily resorted to as a panacea for the mischief already done.

A NARROW ESCAPE

In the township of Musbury there are four or five cottages, known by the name of Park Houses, one of which has been occupied by an elderly man named James Ashworth and his two daughters. It appears that the house in which he resided, was intended to be changed into farm premises, by the addition of a kitchen and cellar at one end of the house, and Ashworth and his daughters had intended removing to another place of residence in consequence. On Tuesday, about noon, the old man and one of his daughters were sitting at the dinner table, when the other daughter ran downstairs, and said she had heard a cracking noise, and believed the house was coming down. The three inmates immediately ran out, apparently just in time to save their lives, for very shortly afterwards the house fell in, burying the furniture in the debris. The family have thus sustained a loss of about £20. Some excavations have been made at the end of the house, deeper than its foundations, for the purpose of making a cellar, and the house not having been shored up, or additionally supported in any way, fell in.

[*Accrington Times 10th October 1868*]

MUSBURY WHISKY

The story of the Grane farmers who brewed their own whisky is well known, but Musbury too had enterprising men and women who decided to supplement their incomes with a bit of home-brewing. James Barlow ('Musbury Jim') was living at Hare Clough in 1881 when he was caught with a whisky still. Two police constables visited the farm in the early hours of 5th July and peering through a window of the front room saw a still built into the fireplace. Through another window they spotted Barlow crouched down watching them. They forced their way into the farmhouse and made a search, finding not only the still but also a network of pipes to supply water, and barrels, tubs and jars containing wash and barm. A channel from the water tub led into the cellar, which was about six inches deep in waste from the still. Standing in front of the discharge pipe of the condenser was a can

James Barlow, the Musbury whisky distiller, (third from left, front row) and his family.
The photograph dates from about 1900 when they were living at Carr Lane.

containing weak whisky, but Barlow later claimed *'It was nowt nobbut water.'* He was
fined £10 and costs.[6]

Musbury Jim later gave his own account of the raid to William Whittaker whose
family made agricultural implements in Accrington.

Tha knows I use to mek a sope o' whisky up yon hollow at Helmshore. I did that an' o' -
it weer gradely stuff too; not t' sooart yo' buy today. And it wur no trouble to get rid on't.
I'd some rare good customers, I hed sooa. I've ta'en mony and mony a gallon to Bury in a
sack on mi back. Wha' mon, I used to fit up o' th' gentry theer at one time. They fairly
liked my whisky, I con tell tha. But they scotched mi cart at last.

Well, one neet, I wur whakened up wi somebody knockin' at t' door. I geet up and
sheawted eawt, "Who's theer?" I head a chap say, "We are Her Majesty's Excise Officers
and we demand admittance."

By gum, that wakken't me, I'll tell tha. I sed to t' wife, "I'm fairly int' kettle this time,
lass." I did some an' wobble going downstairs, for I'd two cream jugs full o' real stuff int'
cellar. Well, I oppened dur, an' three on 'em walked in; then t' foreman said, "We have
reason to believe that you are making whisky illicitly." "Oh, that thinks sooa, dus ta? Well,
hev a look round," I said. But they didn't need telling thad; they were like ferrets i' th'

hoyle, an' they soon fun what they wur after. "Ah, here it is," said one on 'em. I said "Aye, it's theer reet enuf. Will yo' hev a sup just to flush your combs a bit?" "No, thank you, but we must inform you that we shall report what we have found, when, no doubt, you will hear from us again. Good night!"

By gad, thur wur no sleep for me that neet. Th' wife said, "It sarves thi reet." I said "Happen it does. Id'll happen bi mi last brew." An' by gum it wor.

Well, in a day or two I geet a summons to attend at Bury Court at 10 a.m., an' when th' day arrived I wur trudging eawt o' Musbury afoor eight o'clock. Well, I landed at Court at hauf past nine. O' seemed verra quiate, so I crept in an' set mi deawn. In a bit forst one and then another cum in, an' in a bit tooathry bobbies and a bunch o' lawyers cum in wi' their arms full o' papers, an bi 10 o'clock t' court wur nearly full.

Then o' of a sudden a bobby sheawted eawt, "Silence in Court." He fairly med mi jump, but I soon fun eawt what he meant, for o' bobbies and lawyers stood up, and in walked three magistrates and took their seats on t' bench. When I seed 'em I cud hardly believe mi own een. O' th' three on 'em wur owd customers o' mine. But wod med me so mad wor that when them Excise men hed towd ther tale, an' th' magistrates hed whispered to one another a bit, one on 'em stared reight at me an' said, "You are charged with a very grave offence - that of distilling whisky at your farm in Musbury. Don't you think you would have been more profitably employed tilling your farm instead of distilling whisky? It is a very bad case, and we shall fine you £10 and costs, and let this be a lesson to you."

Eh, I wur sum an' mad o' th' time he wur talkin' to me, for th' owd d...l at that verra time hed a full gallon o' my whisky in his cellar. But I thowt I wudn't give th' owd cock away, becose I'd hed mony a good do eawt on him.[7]

Henry Haworth who occupied several farms near Hare Clough in the early 1880s also fell foul of the excise men. On the night of 7th March 1884, several policemen called at Haworth's home at Lower Houses with a search warrant. They found nothing there apart from a two-gallon bottle. Nothing daunted, they pressed on to Higher Hare Clough (also tenanted by Haworth), but again found nothing. Finally, at Haworth's third farm, Ferny Bank, they struck lucky. Their suspicions were aroused when they found water pipes running through several rooms in the building and a flight of stairs that had been partially walled up. From the barn, they climbed through a hole in the wall into a room that smelt strongly of spirits. One of the constables opened a door to reveal the still built into the fireplace. While the search was taking place, one of the neighbours ran to the farm shouting 'Harry, Harry, the police are coming', to which Haworth replied, 'They have been.' He was fined £30 for the possession of the still.[8]

When Johnny Mort spoke to Dr. Tupling in December 1920, he mentioned another whisky distiller. He said he remembered Alice Entwistle who lived at Top o' th' Hillock in the late 1860s making whisky and outwitting the police and excise officers when they came to search her farm.

NOTES

[1] Quarter Session recognizances (LRO: QSB/1/151/24; QSB/1/151/49; QSB/1/151/50)
[2] *Haslingden Observer* 5th February 1927
[3] Dunckley, Henry (ed), *Bamford's Passages in the Life of a Radical and Early Days,* II, (1893), pp. 60 - 62

[4] 1825 6 George IV cap. xcii An act for making and maintaining a road from Bradshaw Brow, near the town of Bolton-le-Moors … to the Bury and Blackburn turnpike road in the township of Haslingden 20th May 1825; Deposited plan for the road (LRO: PDS 31)

[5] Apart from the passage in Dowsett's book, the only other sources on Richmael Smith are her death certificate and the coroner's expense account. (LRO: QSP 3082/250)

[6] *Accrington Times* 17th September 1881

[7] *Haslingden Observer* 23rd April 1927

[8] *Bacup and Rossendale News* 28th April 1884

BIBLIOGRAPHY

MANUSCRIPT SOURCES

The National Archives, London
Census returns for Musbury and Tottington Higher End (HO and RG)
Dissolved companies files (BT31)
Palatinate of Lancaster equity proceedings (PL6)
Tithe files (IR18)

Lancashire Record Office, Preston
Assheton of Downham [Manor of Accrington and Manor of Tottington records] (DDHCL)
Borough of Haslingden (MBH)
Quarter Sessions Recognizances (QSB)
Turnpike road plans (PDS)
Wills (WCW)
Woodcock & Sons, Haslingden (DDX/118)

Manchester Central Library
Farrer manuscripts (L1)

Somerset Record Office
Duckworth of Orchardleigh deeds etc. (DD\DU)

Helmshore Local History Society
Copy of G. H. Tupling's interview notes
Survey of the Helmshore Estate belonging to O. W. Porritt 1922

PRINTED SOURCES

A map or plan of certain proposed reservoirs to be made on or near the River Irwell … (1833) [Rawtenstall Library RC628.13]
Calendar of the Patent Rolls preserved in the Public Record Office 1334 - 1338 (1895)
Farrer, W. (ed), *Lancashire Inquests, Extents, and Feudal Aids, Part II 1310 -1333*, Record Society of Lancashire and Cheshire, 54 (1907)
Farrer, W. (trans), *The Court Rolls of the Honor of Clitheroe*, Volume II (1912); Volume III (1913)
Haslingden Borough Council minutes
Lyons, P. A. (ed), *Two "Compoti" of the Lancashire and Cheshire Manors of Henry de Lacy, Earl of Lincoln, XXIV and XXXIII Edward I*, Chetham Society, Old Series (1884)
Myers, A. R., 'An Official Progress through Lancashire and Cheshire in 1476', *Transactions of the Historic Society of Lancashire and Cheshire*, 115 (1963) 1 - 29
The Thirty Second Annual Report of the Deputy Keeper of the Public Records, Appendix I (1871)
Tupling, G. H. (ed), *South Lancashire in the Reign of Edward II*, Chetham Society, Third Series (1949)

PRINTED SECONDARY WORKS

Aspin, C., *Haslingden 1800 - 1900* (1962)

Beesley, G., *A report of the state of agriculture in Lancashire* (1849)

Brunskill, R. W., *Traditional Farm Buildings of Britain* (1982)

Cantor, L. M. and Hatherly, J., 'The Medieval Parks of England', *Geography*, 64 (1979) 71 - 85

Cunliffe-Shaw, R., *The Royal Forest of Lancaster,* (1956)

Dunckley, H. (ed), *Bamford's Passages in the Life of a Radical and Early Days* (1893)

Hamilton, J. S., 'Henry de Lacy, Fifth Earl of Lincoln', *Oxford Dictionary of National Biography* [Online edition]

Hawkin, R. and Stephens, P., *Historical Notices of Helmshore and Musbury* (1929)

McGarvie, M., 'The Duckworths and the building of Orchardleigh House', *Transactions of the Ancient Monuments Society*, volume 27 (1983) 119 - 145

Marshall Mather, J., *Rambles Round Rossendale* (1888)

Muir, A., *The history of Porritts and Spencer Limited* (1966 typescript)

Rackham, O., *The Illustrated History of the Countryside,* (1994)

TMM (Research) Limited October 1958 (1958)

Tupling, G. H., *The Economic History of Rossendale,* (1927)

Whitaker, T. D., *An History of the Original Parish of Whalley,* 4th edition (1872)

Winchester, A., *The Harvest of the Hills* (2000)

Woodcock, T., *Haslingden. A Topographical History,* Chetham Society, Third Series (1952)

NEWSPAPERS

Accrington Times
Bacup and Rossendale News
Bacup Times
Bolton Chronicle
Burnley Evening Star
Bury Times
Cotton Factory Times
Haslingden and Rawtenstall Express
Haslingden Gazette
Haslingden Guardian
Haslingden Observer
Manchester Mercury
Preston Chronicle
Ramsbottom Observer
Rossendale Free Press
The Times

DIRECTORIES

J. Pigot & Co. *National commercial directory for Cheshire, Cumberland … Lancashire* (1828-9)

INDEX